THE ABUNDANCE CODEX

THE ART OF CREATING YOUR REALITY

COLLEEN GUENTHER

Copyright © 2025 by Colleen Guenther

All rights reserved.

No part of this book may be reproduced in any form or by any electronic or mechanical means, including information storage and retrieval systems, without written permission from the author, except for the use of brief quotations in a book review.

For Justin —
my quiet anchor,
my spiral companion,
and the steady field where my signal remembers itself.
Your presence has been the geometry beneath it all —
the reminder that love doesn't perform,
it resonates.
This book carries your frequency too.

CONTENTS

YOU ARE SOURCE	1
INTRODUCTION	3
HOW TO USE THIS BOOK	5
THE OVERLAY — REMEMBERING WHAT'S REAL	7
PART I — THE CORE DISTORTIONS	11
DISTORTION ZERO — THE FORGOTTEN INTERFACE - BREATHE, BODY AND SIGNAL	12

1. DISTORTION 1: SCARCITY — THE BROADCAST YOU WERE BORN INTO — 16
2. DISTORTION 2: SEPARATION — REMEMBERING — 21
3. DISTORTION 3: NOISE — RECLAIMING YOUR SIGNAL — 26
4. DISTORTION 4: DESERVING — WHY WORTH — 30
5. DISTORTION 5: LINEAR TIME — COLLAPSING THE DELAY — 34
6. DISTORTION 6: HARD WORK — REWRITING THE STRUGGLE CODE — 38
7. DISTORTION 7: PATIENCE — THE INTERNAL DELAY PROGRAM — 42
8. DISTORTION 8: BEING GOOD — BREAKING THE COMPLIANCE SPELL — 46
9. DISTORTION 9: WAITING FOR THE WORLD — THE EXTERNAL PERMISSION LOOP — 50
10. DISTORTION 10: EARNING IT — COLLAPSING THE PROVING LOOP — 54
11. DISTORTION 11: THE WAITING ROOM — WHEN FREEZE MASQUERADES AS SAFETY — 58

PART II — ADVANCED MECHANICS — 62

12. ESCAPE THE BINARY — LIVING BEYOND OPPOSITES — 63
13. RECEIVING IS A SKILL — BECOMING AN OPEN SYSTEM — 66
14. MASTER THE CODES OF CREATION — DIRECTING THE FIELD — 69
15. REWRITE THE IDENTITY GRID — STABILIZING WHO YOU ARE — 72

16. THE BODY BROADCAST — NERVOUS SYSTEM AS FIELD TECHNOLOGY 76
17. YOUR BODY IS THE ANTENNA 79
18. THE PHYSICS OF YOU 81
19. INTEGRATION INSTABILITY — THE OSCILLATION BETWEEN WHO YOU WERE AND WHO YOU ARE BECOMING 83
20. TRUSTING THE FLOW — PRECISION WITHOUT FORCE 87
21. CREATIVE SOVEREIGNTY — EXPRESSING FROM YOUR OVERFLOW 90
    PART III — EMBODIMENT & OVERFLOW 93
22. BUILD THE CONTAINER — HOLDING MORE WITHOUT LEAKS 94
23. THE BODY REMEMBERS — EXPANDING CAPACITY THROUGH PRESENCE 99
24. MONEY LOVES CLARITY — CLEANING THE SIGNAL OF EXCHANGE 103
25. TIME IS WEALTH — RECLAIMING CYCLICAL FLOW 107
26. EXPRESSION MULTIPLIES — MOVING TRUTH THROUGH YOU 110
27. SPEAK WHAT YOU WANT — CODING THE FIELD THROUGH LANGUAGE 113
28. STOP SHRINKING — ALLOWING YOURSELF TO TAKE UP SPACE 117
29. CIRCULATE OR STAGNATE — MOVING ENERGY TO MULTIPLY ENERGY 121
30. YES, RECEIVE MORE — OPENING TO OVERFLOW 124
31. GENEROSITY IS CIRCULATION 127
32. BOUNDARIES PROTECT FLOW — STRUCTURING FOR COHERENCE 130
33. CELEBRATE, DON'T HOARD — LOCKING ABUNDANCE THROUGH JOY 133
    PART IV — FIELD MULTIPLICATION 136
34. SERVICE WITHOUT SAVIORHOOD — SHARING WITHOUT LOSING YOURSELF 137
35. IMPACT THROUGH COHERENCE — STABILIZING COLLECTIVE FIELDS 140
36. ABUNDANCE IS CONTAGIOUS — HOW OVERFLOW SPREADS 143

37. STOP COMPETING — COLLAPSING SCARCITY LOOPS ... 146
38. OTHERS' WINS EXPAND YOU — BECOMING AN AMPLIFIER ... 149
39. COMMUNITY AS WEALTH — BUILDING COHERENT NETWORKS ... 152
40. NON-ATTACHMENT IN ACTION — CREATING WITHOUT CLUTCHING ... 155
41. REST IS PRODUCTIVE — REGENERATION AS MAGNETISM ... 158
42. PLAY CREATES FLOW — UNLOCKING NATURAL EXPANSION ... 161
43. EXPANSION LOVES JOY — FOLLOWING THE FREQUENCY OF EASE ... 164

PART V — FULL EMBODIMENT ... 167

44. DAILY RESET PRACTICES — RETURNING TO SIGNAL FAST ... 168
45. MICRO-ABUNDANCE CHOICES — SMALL SHIFTS, MASSIVE RIPPLE ... 171
46. ANCHOR ABUNDANCE IN YOUR SPACE — DESIGNING YOUR FIELD ... 174
47. ABUNDANCE IN LOVE — RECEIVING WITHOUT COLLAPSE ... 177
48. ABUNDANCE IN WORK — CREATING BEYOND SURVIVAL ... 180
49. ABUNDANCE IN ART — OPENING CREATIVE CHANNELS ... 184
50. ABUNDANCE IN HEALTH — COHERENCE IN THE BODY ... 187
51. HOLDING BIGGER FIELDS — EXPANDING WITHOUT BURNOUT ... 190
52. ABUNDANCE AS BASELINE — STABILIZING OVERFLOW AS NORMAL ... 193
53. LIVING THE OVERFLOW — BECOMING THE SOURCE ... 197
54. LIVING THE FIELD — SIGNAL-BASED REALITY IN REAL TIME ... 201
55. THE FIELD REMEMBERS YOU ... 205

CLOSING NOTES ... 209
INTEGRATION REFLECTIONS ... 211

About the Author ... 213

YOU ARE SOURCE

Before the roles.
    Before the rules.
    Before the noise of who you were taught to be.
You were Source.
Whole. Infinite. Untouched by lack.
You are everything you've been searching for — and the point of this life is to remember.

This world is designed for forgetting.

You enter through overlays — family stories, cultural rules, religious control, educational scripts — each layer pulling you further from the truth of what you are.

They teach you survival.
They teach you hierarchy.
They teach you scarcity.

And yet, beneath all the programming, the signal has never left you.

The forgetting isn't a mistake. It's the design.

Consciousness chooses to experience itself through limitation so that remembering becomes **embodied**, not conceptual.

Life isn't testing you.

Life is revealing you.

Source wants to experience itself **through you** — through your lens, your desires, your body, your creations, your frequency.

You are the interface between infinite potential and physical reality.

Every thought you hold, every boundary you set, every signal you stabilize — all of it codes the geometry of your life.

When you forget, you loop.

When you remember, you create.

This book exists for one reason: to bring you back to the remembering.

Not as an idea — but as an experience you live in your body.

You are not separate from the field.

You are not separate from what you want.

You are the Source that creates it.

And when you remember, reality remembers you.

INTRODUCTION

This book isn't here to give you a strategy.
It's here to tune you back to yourself.
You don't need to "learn" abundance, coherence, or overflow.
You already are the signal.
The Abundance Codex is simply a tool to help you stabilize it — to dissolve distortion, drop the overlays, and let the field organize around your clarity.
Signal-Based Living™ isn't a framework.
It's not a method to master, a checklist to follow, or a mindset to "fake."
It's the physics of creation — living from the frequency beneath the noise, where your choices, your body, and your reality align without force.
This isn't about "manifesting" something you don't have.
It's about remembering what's already yours.
When your nervous system stabilizes safety, when your thoughts, emotions, and actions broadcast one coherent signal, reality reorganizes itself naturally.
Not because you performed enough, earned enough, or proved enough.

But because you stopped scrambling the geometry.
You don't become abundant.
You remember you already are.

HOW TO USE THIS BOOK

This book isn't linear.

It's alive.

You don't have to start at page one, follow the chapters in order, or "complete" the material before it works. You can open to any page, any section, any FIELD IN MOTION example, and you'll land exactly where your system needs to stabilize.

Inside, you'll find six core mechanics woven through every chapter:

• **Frequency** — The tone your system broadcasts into the field, consciously or unconsciously. It organizes reality around you.

• **Coherence** — Alignment between what you think, feel, choose, and broadcast. When your internal signal matches your external expression, the field mirrors it instantly.

• **The Field** — The larger energetic web of timelines and possibilities constantly responding to your signal.

• **Signal** — Your unique energetic blueprint. The more you stabilize your tone, the faster reality reorganizes in your favor.

• **Overlay** — A collective program or borrowed rule-set (like linear time, deserving, or scarcity) layered over the field. Overlays distort geometry — coherence restores it.

- **Geometry** — The way energy organizes itself around belief and broadcast. Distortion scrambles it. Stabilization brings it back online.

EVERYTHING in this book moves through one living truth: **your signal shapes the field.** The field isn't abstract — it's a **living web of energy and geometry** constantly responding to what you believe, feel, and broadcast. When your internal world is coherent, the geometry of your life organizes into clarity, flow, and synchronicity. When distortion enters — fear, scarcity, borrowed rules — the geometry scrambles, and reality feels heavy or stuck. **This book shows you how to restore your natural pattern** so that life reorganizes around your clearest signal, effortlessly and without force.

THE **FIELD IN MOTION** sections are your living examples. They show exactly how these mechanics translate into real life — where shifting one choice, one tone, one signal creates ripple effects in the field.

This isn't a book you read once and shelve. It's a companion — something you return to when your system feels stuck, heavy, or unclear. Every time you re-enter, you'll hear something new — because your signal will be ready to receive more.

Take your time. Pause when something lands. Come back to chapters that feel sticky, charged, or alive. Let the book move with you as your frequency evolves.

Because you don't have to "become" anything.
You're remembering what's already here.
You are the Source.
Everything begins from there.

THE OVERLAY — REMEMBERING WHAT'S REAL

Humanity has been living inside a carefully designed illusion — a multi-layered system built to keep you disconnected from your power, distracted from your true nature, and obedient to rules you never chose.

This is what I call **the overlay.**

It touches nearly everything: how you're educated, governed, conditioned — even what you believe about love, success, safety, and God.

But here's the truth:

The overlay is not reality.

It's a framework of control — and waking up begins the moment you see it.

THE SYSTEM THAT SHAPED YOU

From the moment you were born, you were placed inside structures designed to make you forget who you are and what you're capable of.

. . .

GOVERNMENT → CONTROL THROUGH FEAR

Governments weren't created to "protect freedom."

They were designed to manage populations and control resources.

• Laws and policies dictate what's allowed — not what's true.

• Power is centralized, conditioning you to believe authority lives outside you.

• Division is deliberate: right vs. left, us vs. them.

• Constant conflict keeps you distracted from questioning the structure itself.

When people are afraid, divided, and dependent, they're easier to control.

EDUCATION → TRAINING OBEDIENCE, NOT FREEDOM

Schools weren't built to unlock your potential — they were designed to produce predictable workers during the Industrial Revolution.

• Bells train you to move on someone else's schedule.

• Memorization is prioritized over critical thinking.

• Creativity is suppressed; conformity is rewarded.

From childhood, you're taught to look outside yourself for answers, permission, and authority. You're trained to perform, not to question.

RELIGION → SEPARATION FROM SOURCE

Religion wasn't designed to bring you closer to God — it was built to mediate your access to the divine.

• You're taught you are broken and must earn salvation.

• Spiritual authority is outsourced to priests, pastors, or institutions.

• Fear of punishment — heaven vs. hell — keeps you compliant.

But here's the deeper truth:

You are Source expressing through form.

No one can grant or revoke your divinity.

As long as people believe God lives "somewhere else," they remain bound to systems promising access to what was never missing.

MEDIA & TECHNOLOGY → PROGRAMMING THE NARRATIVE

Mass media doesn't exist to tell the truth — it exists to shape perception.

- Stories are curated to control collective focus — keeping people fearful, outraged, or distracted.
- Attention becomes currency. If you're busy reacting to headlines, you're not creating your reality.
- Algorithms amplify distortion, locking people into echo chambers where consensus reality feels inescapable.

When the mind is overstimulated and divided, the signal stays off.

MONEY & SYSTEMS OF SCARCITY

The financial system is one of the deepest overlays — designed to keep you chasing survival instead of creating from freedom.

- Debt traps individuals and nations in cycles of lack.
- The myth of finite resources drives constant competition.
- People trade time, energy, and creativity just to stay afloat — never questioning why abundance feels so far away.

Scarcity isn't natural.

It's manufactured to keep humanity looping in survival mode — disconnected from the infinite nature of the field.

THE MOMENT OF REMEMBERING

Then something happens — a crack in the story.

You start noticing patterns.

You realize the rules you've been living by are **constructed, not natural**.

This is the moment of remembering:
- You are not broken.
- You are not separate.
- You are not powerless inside these systems.

You are **Source**, expressed uniquely, and you've been this all along.

Remembering isn't about learning something new — it's about seeing through the illusion designed to make you forget.

THE DOORWAY THIS BOOK OPENS

The overlay exists to keep you looping in scarcity, separation, and survival.

But this book isn't about fighting those systems.

It's about remembering what's **true beyond them** — and stabilizing your signal in a reality where the overlay no longer defines you.

Every distortion that follows is a doorway.

Each one dissolves a layer of programming, returning you to what's always been yours: your clarity, your power, and your original coherence.

You're not here to escape the world.

You're here to **move differently inside it.**

To stop playing by rules that were never yours.

To reclaim the signal you've always carried.

From here, the rest of the codex becomes your field guide — a map for dissolving distortion and creating abundantly beyond the illusion.

PART I — THE CORE DISTORTIONS

Rewriting the foundation: dismantling the distortions that collapse your field

DISTORTION ZERO — THE FORGOTTEN INTERFACE - BREATHE, BODY AND SIGNAL

The Breath, The Body, The Signal
You've been taught to "fix your mindset." To think better thoughts.
To visualize harder.
To control reality from the neck up.
But thought alone can't collapse distortion.
You cannot exit loops through the mind.
Because the mind isn't the command center — **your nervous system is.**

Every broadcast you send into the field — abundance or lack, safety or fear, expansion or contraction — runs through the body first.

- When the body braces, the field mirrors scarcity back.
- When the body relaxes, timelines open and reality reorganizes instantly.

This is the missing key:
Your body is the interface.
Your breath is the control panel.
Your nervous system is the tuner for your signal.

. . .

The Body Holds the Program

Distortion isn't just "beliefs." It's biology.

- If your family coded survival as safety, your body learned to stay small.
- If school trained you to compete for worth, your system learned to chase approval.
- If love came with conditions, your breath learned to shallow and grip.

These codes aren't wrong — they were inherited survival strategies.

But when the nervous system never learns another way, it rejects overflow automatically — no matter how much your conscious mind "knows" the field is infinite.

This is why more knowledge won't free you.

Your body has to **remember safety** before your reality can reorganize.

Breath Is the Bridge

Breath is how you rewrite the program.

- Inhale slowly → tell your system: *I'm safe here.*
- Exhale fully → signal: *It's safe to hold more now.*

Every long, regulated breath codes your biology for expansion.

Every grounded pause resets timelines your mind thought were fixed.

This isn't "breathwork" as performance.

This is coherence in motion — the portal where thought and biology unify into one transmission.

Micro-Protocol: 20-Second Reset

Use this whenever you feel scattered, overwhelmed, or drifting:

- Inhale for **4 seconds** → silently say: "Safe."
- Exhale for **6 seconds** → silently say: "Open."
- Repeat for **3–4 rounds**.

By the third breath, your nervous system begins unhooking from survival mode.

By the fourth, your signal clears.

The field doesn't respond to how hard you try — it responds to how deeply you stabilize.

The Mechanics of Capacity

Overflow doesn't land because you "call it in."

It lands because your body learns to hold it.

- When the body braces → timelines constrict.
- When the body relaxes → possibilities multiply.
- When safety codes in → the field reorganizes around you.

Your nervous system decides how much love, money, freedom, and visibility you allow — often without you realizing it.

Every conscious breath expands your capacity, one cycle at a time.

Activation

Speak this aloud:

"I return to my body.

I breathe safety into my system.

I open space to hold more.

My signal stabilizes through my breath.

I remember: overflow lives here, now."

Pause.

Place both feet flat on the floor and press gently into them.

Feel your body anchor into the now.

Let your system register the remembering.

Field in Motion

You're spiraling — over a launch, a decision, a relationship.

The mind races, the body grips, the signal scatters.

You pause.

Close your eyes.
Inhale four seconds: safe.
Exhale six seconds: open.
Within a minute, your chest softens.
The urgency dissolves.
An idea drops in.
The next step becomes obvious.
Nothing outside you changed.
Your breath recoded the field from the inside out.

1

DISTORTION 1: SCARCITY — THE BROADCAST YOU WERE BORN INTO

Scarcity isn't real.

It's a broadcast — a distortion you were born into.

From the moment you arrived, systems trained your nervous system to collapse into limitation:

- Education measured worth by compliance, not curiosity.
- Work rewarded exhaustion, not coherence.
- Religion delayed heaven until "later."
- Media sold fear so you'd keep consuming.

Scarcity was never designed to protect you.

It was engineered to keep you small, performing, and dependent on systems that profit when you forget your original signal.

The Broadcast Mechanics

Scarcity operates like a signal jam inside your field:

You believe something's missing → The body braces → Energy contracts → Timelines slow → The field mirrors that back.

You chase.

You prove.

You compete.

You collapse.
But the deeper truth: **nothing has ever been missing.**
Abundance has always been the baseline code.
Scarcity only exists where it's believed.

The Body Remembers

Scarcity isn't just an idea in your head — it's stored in your nervous system.

If your body learned that having more wasn't safe, it will unconsciously reject overflow — no matter how much your conscious mind "knows" the field is infinite.

This is why knowing the principles of abundance isn't enough.

You can't "think" your way into receiving.

You have to **teach the body safety again** — to hold more, rest deeper, and expand into what you already are.

Nature Remembers

Look at the natural field:

- A tree doesn't negotiate how many leaves it will grow. It grows until there's no more room to give.
- Rivers don't hold back their currents. They move, replenish, return.
- The sun doesn't save its warmth for later. It radiates fully, knowing there's always more.

Life doesn't perform scarcity.

It multiplies. Everywhere. Always.

The only place scarcity exists is in the human mind — and in the systems built from that distortion.

Where the Program Came From

Scarcity isn't yours.

It's inherited — running in silent loops from:

- Family systems → rules about safety, worth, and survival
- Cultural narratives → stories equating sacrifice with virtue
- Economic frameworks → structures designed to create dependency
- Collective programming → the global hum of "not enough" embedded in nearly every institution

Once you see it, you can't unsee it.

Scarcity isn't truth.

It's conditioning.

Rewriting the Script

Scarcity hides inside "rational" behaviors — like overworking, hoarding, comparing, or waiting until you feel "ready." These loops send one message to the field: **I can't hold more.**

But your signal is stronger than the program.

You rewrite the code when you stabilize a new tone:

- Instead of saying, *"I need to earn it,"* you anchor into, *"I normalize receiving with ease."*
- Instead of believing, *"There's not enough,"* you embody, *"The field always circulates more."*
- Instead of thinking, *"If they win, I lose,"* you hold, *"Their expansion codes mine."*
- Instead of waiting with, *"I'll celebrate when I have it,"* you broadcast, *"I stabilize joy now."*

This isn't about forcing "positive thinking."

It's about sending your body a signal it can trust — one that reorganizes the field from the inside out.

Pause here.

Take one slow, grounded breath.

Let the rewritten code land in your body — don't just think it.

Creating New Realities

When you stop feeding the distortion, entirely new geometries open:
- Opportunities appear where you once saw limitation.
- Money circulates without gripping or force.
- Relationships deepen as comparison dissolves.
- Your body relaxes, creating capacity to receive more.

Overflow isn't something you "call in."

It's what remains when you stop broadcasting lack.

Activation

Speak this aloud:

"Scarcity is not mine.

I revoke the broadcast.

I walk in surplus.

I breathe in overflow.

I stabilize the geometry of enough."

Pause.

Rest one hand on your **belly** and the other over your **heart**.

Let your inhale rise under your bottom hand and your exhale soften under the top hand.

Feel your body register the geometry of **enough**.

Field in Motion

You've been hesitating to sign up for a class that excites you.

Old programming whispers:

"Wait until you have more money."

"Wait until you're ready."

"Be safe."

This time, you pause.

You drop into your body.

You listen.

It's a yes.

You register — not from force, not to "earn" something, but to expand into it now.

The next week, your energy shifts.

You feel lighter, more open, more alive — and small synchronicities begin flowing in:

a new idea drops, a conversation sparks, an unexpected opportunity lands.

The return didn't come from the class.

It came from **changing the broadcast** — stabilizing trust in your capacity to hold more, now.

2

DISTORTION 2: SEPARATION — REMEMBERING

The Lie of "Me" vs. "Everything Else"
From the moment you were born, you were taught a story:

You are a separate person.

In a separate body.

With separate needs.

In a separate world.

This story is so deep, most people never question it.

As mentioned in the beginning of the book, it runs in education, religion, economics, medicine, and politics — a collective hum that says:

"You are small. You are powerless. The answers are out there, not in here."

But here's the truth:

You were never separate.

You are **Source** expressing itself through form.

Your body isn't the edge of you — it's the interface of the infinite.

When you collapse the separation, everything changes.

. . .

The Mechanics of Separation

Separation is the distortion that creates all others.

It whispers: *"There's a gap between you and what you want."*

- Between you and God.
- Between you and love.
- Between you and safety.
- Between you and abundance.

But there is **no gap:**

- The frequency of what you want already exists.
- Your signal — your thoughts, your breath, your field — is how you tune into it.
- The "waiting," the "earning," the "not enough" — those are programs layered on top of what's already here.

You're not calling reality to you.

You're remembering what you already are.

The Illusion of Control

Separation teaches you that life is happening *to* you, and so you try to manage it:

You force.

You chase.

You grip timelines, trying to control the outcome.

But control is always rooted in fear.

It assumes you're cut off from the field, alone, unsupported.

It broadcasts lack — and the field mirrors that lack back.

When you remember you are Source, control dissolves into trust.

You no longer manipulate outcomes; you **stabilize alignment.**

Reality arranges to match your tone.

Coming Home to the Field

The field is not outside you.

It **is you.**

It's the living intelligence you're woven from — the same consciousness that holds stars, rivers, and trees in coherence.

When you stabilize into your own signal, you return to this knowing.

You no longer need to "get" anything.

You let what already exists find its way into form **through you**.

How Separation Shows Up

Separation hides inside tiny, everyday patterns:
- Comparing your pace to someone else's and collapsing into "behind"
- Believing God, safety, or love are "out there" to find
- Feeling disconnected from your purpose, power, or capacity
- Chasing experiences to "become whole" instead of remembering you already are

The field mirrors your inner tone.

When your body trusts there's **no gap**, life stops performing scarcity.

Rewriting the Script

Separation dissolves the moment you stabilize this remembering:
You are the field.

What you seek is made of the same frequency you are.
- Instead of believing, *"I need to go out there and get it,"* you hold, *"I broadcast it, so it organizes around me."*
- Instead of thinking, *"I'll feel safe when I arrive,"* you embody, *"I stabilize safety now."*
- Instead of collapsing into, *"They have what I don't,"* you breathe into, *"Their expansion codes mine."*
- Instead of seeking God "up there," you remember, *"God breathes as me, through me, within me."*

This isn't a concept for your mind to "figure out."

It's a truth your body already knows.
Pause.
Breathe.
Feel the edge between "me" and "everything else" blur, dissolve, and unify.

Activation
Speak this aloud:
"I am Source remembering itself.
There is no gap.
I relax the grip on control.
I stabilize my belonging.
What I seek, I already am."
Pause.
Close your eyes and widen your **peripheral vision** slowly — letting your awareness stretch beyond the edges of your body.
Feel your boundaries soften.
Let your nervous system experience the "no-gap" signal directly.

Field in Motion
You're standing at the edge of a big decision — changing careers, moving cities, leaving a relationship.
The mind spirals:
"What if I make the wrong choice?"
"What if I lose stability?"
"What if I'm not supported?"
You pause.
One deep breath.
Peripheral vision widens.
A sense of spaciousness fills your body.
You remember: there is no "out there."
The field is not separate from you.
Suddenly, the next step becomes obvious.

The choice isn't about risk or safety anymore — it's about alignment.
You don't "get" the right outcome.
You **broadcast** the right outcome.
The field organizes around your coherence.

3

DISTORTION 3: NOISE — RECLAIMING YOUR SIGNAL

The Static That Scrambles Your Signal
You're designed to receive clarity.
To sense your next step without forcing it.
To feel the signal beneath the noise.
But the world you were born into runs on distraction.
Your nervous system is constantly flooded with notifications, opinions, algorithms, headlines, and agendas — all designed to fragment your attention and scatter your energy.
Noise is not neutral.
It scrambles the broadcast.
When your field is jammed, you can't hear your own frequency — so you end up chasing someone else's.

How Noise Enters the System

Noise isn't just external.
It's every place you've internalized the hum of "should," "must," and "not enough."
- Scrolling feeds that tell you how far behind you are
- Comparing your pace to someone else's

- Listening to conflicting advice instead of your own clarity
- Forcing productivity because "rest isn't safe"
- Taking on other people's fears, doubts, and timelines

Every unfiltered input becomes a signal your body tries to process.

But your capacity isn't infinite — if you don't choose what enters, the field chooses for you.

The Mechanics of Clarity

Your reality organizes around the loudest frequency in your field.

When noise dominates, your broadcast fragments — you start leaking energy, losing presence, and doubting your own knowing.

But when you clear noise, coherence returns:
- You move from force to flow.
- Decisions become obvious instead of overwhelming.
- Synchronicities increase because you can hear the next step.

Noise doesn't just drown out your intuition.

It keeps you looping in timelines that don't belong to you.

Choosing Signal Over Static

You don't control the noise in the world.

You control your broadcast **inside** it.

That's what tuning is — choosing which frequencies you allow in, and which ones you dissolve.

Every choice to curate your inputs, breathe before reacting, or pause before responding clears static from your field.

Noise can't exist where presence lives.

Stillness amplifies your signal more than effort ever could.

How to Notice the Noise

A simple tell:

If you feel overwhelmed, confused, or restless, there's noise in your field.

Your clarity is never truly missing — it's just buried beneath layers of unprocessed inputs.

When you stop feeding the static, your original signal comes online.

Remember: the field organizes around what you stabilize.

When you stabilize stillness, reality gets quieter too.

Rewriting the Script

Noise dissolves when you shift the tone of your broadcast:

- Instead of saying, *"I need more information before I decide,"* you breathe into, *"Clarity lives in me now."*
- Instead of thinking, *"I'm behind,"* you hold, *"I move in perfect timing."*
- Instead of collapsing into, *"Everyone else knows better,"* you remember, *"I trust my own signal first."*
- Instead of spiraling in, *"I need to do more,"* you stabilize, *"I create more by receiving more."*

These aren't affirmations.

They're instructions — commands your body, breath, and field can actually register.

Activation

Speak this aloud:

"I quiet the static.

I return to presence.

My signal is clear.

My next step arrives with ease."

Pause.

Soften your **jaw** and **lengthen your exhale** slowly until your breath feels quieter than your thoughts.

Feel your system settle into stillness as your signal rises to the surface.

Field in Motion

You open your laptop to finish a project.

Within minutes, you've checked your messages, scrolled through three apps, and compared yourself to five strangers.

Now your body feels tight, your mind scattered, and your energy drained.

You pause.

Close the tabs.

Set the phone down.

Soften your jaw.

Exhale fully.

Within seconds, you feel the shift.

The tension eases.

You hear the one action to take next — the one that moves the entire project forward.

It was never missing.

Your signal was just buried beneath the static.

4

DISTORTION 4: DESERVING — WHY WORTH

The Myth of Worthiness
From the moment you could walk, you were taught that your value had to be earned:
- Earn love by behaving.
- Earn safety by performing.
- Earn belonging by fitting in.
- Earn rest by exhausting yourself first.

Every system you've been inside — family, school, work, religion — reinforced one message:

"You're not enough yet. Do more. Be better. Prove it."

But here's the truth:

You were **born enough.**

Nothing you do can add to your worth — and nothing you fail to do can take it away.

The Program of Deserving

Deserving is one of the deepest distortions in the human field.

It whispers:

"You can't have what you want until you've suffered enough to earn it."

And so you wait.

You overperform.

You chase approval.

You shrink your desires to what feels "reasonable."

But the field doesn't measure worth.

It mirrors **signal**.

If your body believes love, freedom, or abundance must be earned, the field will reflect delay — until you update the code.

What Happens in the Body

Deserving isn't just an idea — it's wired into your nervous system.

- When you've learned love is conditional, the body braces before receiving it.
- When safety came from proving, your breath locks before rest.
- When visibility once carried shame, your chest tightens before being seen.

This is why you can "know" you're worthy and still feel blocked.

Until your body registers safety, your reality keeps playing the old program on repeat.

The Inheritance

The deserving distortion isn't personal — it's collective.

It came from:

- Generations conditioned to tie survival to proving
- Institutions equating sacrifice with virtue
- Cultural stories that glorify suffering as the price of worthiness

You were born into it.

And now, you get to end it.

Rewriting the Script

Deserving dissolves the moment you stabilize a different broadcast:

- Instead of thinking, *"I have to earn this,"* you breathe into, *"I receive with ease."*
- Instead of fearing, *"I'll be judged if I want more,"* you hold, *"My desires are instructions from the field."*
- Instead of collapsing into, *"Others are more worthy than me,"* you embody, *"I was born enough."*
- Instead of waiting for proof, you stabilize, *"I normalize having it now."*

This isn't about affirmations.

It's about instructing your body and breath to send a signal your reality can organize around.

Pause here.

Let your shoulders drop.

Feel this remembering settle deeper than thought.

Living **Beyond Deserving**

When you collapse the "deserving" distortion:

- You stop waiting for permission.
- Receiving stops feeling dangerous.
- Overflow becomes your baseline, not a reward.
- You expand your capacity to hold more without bracing.

The field responds to what you stabilize, not what you think you've "earned."

When you broadcast safety in receiving, the timelines accelerate.

Activation

Speak this aloud:

"I was born enough.

My worth is not earned.

I open to receive with ease.

I stabilize the signal of already."

Pause.

Close your eyes and bring your awareness to your **shoulder blades**.

Soften them downward.

Let your upper body rest heavy, signaling your system that it's safe to **receive without proving**.

Field in Motion

You're considering raising your rates — a number that actually reflects the value of your work.

But an old loop surfaces:

"Who am I to charge that?"

"Will anyone even pay it?"

"Am I good enough yet?"

You pause.

Close your eyes.

Two slow breaths: open, steady.

You remember: you're not "earning" value — you're **matching your external reality** to the worth that's always been there.

You raise your rates without gripping.

The next client comes in with a yes before you even pitch.

It wasn't the price that shifted.

It was the **broadcast**.

5

DISTORTION 5: LINEAR TIME — COLLAPSING THE DELAY

The Trap of "Later"
You were taught to live in timelines:
First this, then that.
Work hard now, enjoy life later.
Prove yourself first, rest later.
Sacrifice today, receive tomorrow.
Linear time conditions you to delay your own expansion.
It programs you to believe that what you want lives "out there" — in the future — instead of here, now.
But the truth is simpler:
Reality isn't linear.
Time bends around frequency.
When your signal stabilizes, timelines reorganize instantly.

HOW THE LOOP Works

Linear time creates a false gap:
- Between where you are and where you "should" be
- Between who you are and who you want to become

- Between your desire and your capacity to hold it

That gap makes you wait for permission.

It makes you believe your future self is the one who "deserves" it — not you, here, now.

But the field doesn't work like that.

Your signal shapes what arrives — and the signal is now.

Not tomorrow.

Not when you're "ready."

Now.

THE GEOMETRY of Now

When you drop out of linear time, you step into coherence:

- Possibilities multiply
- Synchronicities accelerate
- Things arrive without the grind, the chase, or the delay

What looks like "miracles" are just geometry responding to stabilized frequency.

Linear time collapses when you remember: your field isn't on a clock.

REWRITING the Script

Linear time dissolves when you stop broadcasting delay and stabilize presence instead:

- Instead of thinking, "I'm not there yet," you breathe into, **"I arrive now."**
- Instead of spiraling in, "It'll take years to get there," you hold, **"My timelines reorganize around my signal."**
- Instead of believing, "I'll feel abundant when it happens," you embody, **"I feel abundant now, so it happens."**
- Instead of waiting for "someday," you stabilize, **"The moment I choose, the field moves."**

These aren't affirmations — they're instructions.

You're teaching your body to stop holding reality at arm's length.

ANCHORING the Frequency

This isn't about bypassing real-world action.

It's about collapsing the energetic delay that keeps you in holding patterns.

When your body believes abundance lives "later," it blocks receiving now.

When your breath stabilizes safety in this moment, your field reorganizes around it.

Timelines accelerate when the nervous system stops bracing.

ACTIVATION

Speak this aloud:

"I exit the waiting game.

I collapse the illusion of delay.

My signal moves reality now.

I stabilize here, where everything already lives."

Pause.

Place both feet on the floor and press your toes gently into the ground.

Feel the weight drop into your heels as you whisper, **"I arrive now."**

Let your body anchor into the geometry of present time.

FIELD IN MOTION

You've been avoiding a difficult conversation with your partner, telling yourself you'll bring it up "when the timing is right."

Each day, the tension builds.

The future moment never comes.

Today, you pause.

Feet grounded.

Three slow breaths — safe, open, here.
You start the conversation.
You speak from steadiness instead of urgency.
To your surprise, the exchange moves with ease.
Clarity arrives. Connection opens.
The timeline didn't heal with waiting.
It reorganized the moment you entered it.

6

DISTORTION 6: HARD WORK — REWRITING THE STRUGGLE CODE

The Programming of Grind

From childhood, you were taught to worship effort:
- Work harder than everyone else
- Hustle now, enjoy life later
- Push, prove, achieve, repeat

The grind was framed as noble — the pathway to worth, safety, and success.

But beneath it, the message was simple:

"If you stop producing, you stop deserving."

Hard work became the currency for belonging.

And somewhere along the way, your nervous system learned that exhaustion equals value.

The Trap of Over-performance

Here's what happens inside the field when you over-perform:
- The body braces.
- Your energy leaks into timelines that don't belong to you.
- The signal you send says: *"I must work harder to have more."*

And the field mirrors that instruction back — keeping you in the very loop you're trying to escape.

This is why no amount of grinding ever feels like "enough."

The program was never designed to lead you to overflow.

It was designed to keep you producing **without arriving**.

When Action Becomes Aligned

This isn't about rejecting effort — it's about rejecting distortion.

There's a difference between working hard from force and moving from alignment:

- **Force drains you.** Alignment restores you.
- **Force fights the field.** Alignment flows with it.
- **Force works for worth.** Alignment creates from enoughness.

Aligned action feels lighter.

It doesn't push; it **pulls**.

You don't make reality happen — you stabilize your signal so reality reorganizes around it.

The Nervous System Shift

Your body has likely been conditioned to associate effort with safety.

That means even when the aligned path appears, your system might still grip, doubt, or over-perform to "earn it."

The shift begins here:
- Let your breath anchor safety first.
- Move when your body feels open, not tight.
- Let receiving feel as normal as giving.

When your nervous system trusts ease, overflow lands without force.

Rewriting the Script

Hard work dissolves when you broadcast a different instruction:

- Instead of thinking, *"If I slow down, I'll fall behind,"* you breathe into, *"The field moves when I do."*
- Instead of believing, *"I must hustle to deserve it,"* you hold, *"My signal organizes reality without strain."*
- Instead of collapsing into, *"I don't have enough yet,"* you embody, *"Overflow lives here, now."*
- Instead of forcing outcomes, you stabilize, *"Alignment is more powerful than effort."*

This isn't about doing less.

It's about moving **differently**.

When your tone shifts, the timelines shift.

Activation

Speak this aloud:

"I release the grind.

I stabilize ease.

I trust aligned action.

Overflow responds to my signal, not my struggle."

Pause.

Rest both hands on your **thighs**.

Feel the weight of your palms grounding you into stillness.

Let the body register that you are safe, stable, and allowed to move from **sufficiency**, not effort.

Field in Motion

You've been saying yes to every opportunity, believing hard work will finally "get you there."

You're exhausted — stretched, scattered, and out of sync.

One morning, you wake up and pause before touching your phone.

You sit.

Hands on thighs.

Three slow breaths: safe, open, here.

From that stillness, you feel it clearly: one thing matters today.
You follow that thread.
The action flows easily — and creates more impact than a week of hustling ever did.
You didn't work harder.
You worked **in alignment**.
That's the shift.

7

DISTORTION 7: PATIENCE — THE INTERNAL DELAY PROGRAM

The Virtue Program
You were taught patience as a virtue:
"Good things come to those who wait."
"Be patient — your time will come."
"Don't rush; you're not ready yet."

But in the field, patience is often a disguise for delay energy — keeping you stuck in holding patterns, bracing for permission to arrive.

You weren't born patient.
You were taught to suppress your own timing.

HOW PATIENCE BECOMES a Cage
Patience creates subtle forms of self-abandonment:
- Waiting until you "deserve" it
- Waiting until it feels safe
- Waiting until confidence arrives
- Waiting until every internal signal feels perfect

Underneath patience, there's often fear — fear of being seen, fear of failing, fear of trusting your own signal.

Patience becomes the way we justify staying small: "I'll move when I'm ready."

But readiness isn't something you wait for.

It's something you stabilize.

THE NOW FREQUENCY

The field doesn't respond to patience.

It responds to presence.

When you stabilize safety now, your energy reorganizes, timelines open, and aligned opportunities appear without force.

You stop waiting to arrive — because you realize you're already standing in the place you thought you needed to get to.

Patience keeps you holding your breath for a better future.

Presence lets you breathe it here.

CERTAINTY — THE GUARANTEE ILLUSION

Certainty is control dressed as safety. It sounds wise — "Wait until you're sure." But it's just delay energy in nicer clothes.

The field doesn't move on guarantees. It moves on stabilized signal.

When you demand proof first → the body braces → perception narrows → timing stalls → "no evidence" appears → you wait longer.

REWRITING the Script

Patience dissolves when you replace delayed belonging with immediate coherence:

- Instead of thinking, "It's not my time yet," you hold, **"I'm in my timing now."**
- Instead of believing, "I'll move when the conditions are right," you breathe into, **"I create the conditions by choosing."**
- Instead of saying, "I'll feel safe once I arrive," you embody, **"Safety codes in when I relax here."**

- Instead of whispering, "Someday," you stabilize, **"Today holds everything I was waiting for."**

This isn't about forcing action.

It's about ending the posture of postponement so your signal aligns with the field in real time.

ENDING the Performance of Patience

Patience was never your natural state — it was programmed into you to control your timing.

When you release it, you open access to:
- Decisions that land clean and clear
- Overflow that doesn't require proving or waiting
- Synchronicities that arrive faster than the mind believes possible

The illusion isn't that you have to wait.

The illusion is that anything is missing.

ACTIVATION

Speak this aloud:

"I exit the posture of waiting.

I choose my timing now.

My breath collapses delay."

The field reorganizes as I do.

Rest the tip of your tongue gently on the roof of your mouth as you breathe.

Feel the circuit complete — grounding you fully into your body and stabilizing your signal in the present moment.

FIELD IN MOTION

You've been sitting on your artwork for months, telling yourself you'll share it "when the time is right."

Weeks pass. Then months.

Each day, you feel the pull — but you keep postponing, thinking alignment will come from outside you.

One morning, you pause.

Tongue resting softly in place.

Three slow breaths.

A calm certainty lands: the waiting isn't protecting you — it's pausing you.

You post the work.

Within hours, someone reaches out. They want to collaborate.

The energy shifts instantly — not because the timing magically arrived,

but because you stopped outsourcing your timing to the future.

8

DISTORTION 8: BEING GOOD — BREAKING THE COMPLIANCE SPELL

The Obedience Code
From the moment you arrived, you were taught to be **good**:
- Good students get gold stars.
- Good children get love.
- Good employees get raises.
- Good citizens follow the rules.

"Good" became the currency of belonging.

Your body learned to **perform approval** to stay safe, loved, and included.

But here's the distortion:

Being good isn't the same as **being true**.

The Cost of Performing

When you trade authenticity for acceptance, you send a distorted broadcast into the field. It says:

"Who I really am isn't enough."

And so you hide parts of yourself.

You shrink to avoid disapproval.

You suppress desires that might make others uncomfortable.

The problem is, the more you contort to be "good," the further you drift from your **natural frequency** — and the harder it becomes to hear your own signal.

Goodness can't stabilize overflow.

Truth can.

The Hidden Root

This programming didn't start with you.

It was passed down:
- Families using love as leverage
- Schools rewarding obedience over curiosity
- Religions equating morality with compliance
- Institutions punishing individuality to maintain control

The result?

A nervous system coded to believe that safety lives **outside of you** — in the opinions, reactions, and validations of others.

When "Good" Becomes the Distraction

Performing goodness fragments your energy:
- You say yes when your body screams no
- You soften your voice to avoid confrontation
- You dim your light so others feel comfortable
- You choose "safe" paths over the ones that feel alive

Every time you abandon yourself to perform safety, your field mirrors it back as stagnation, scarcity, and exhaustion.

Freedom arrives the moment you decide **approval is optional.**

Rewriting the Script

Being good dissolves when you stabilize authenticity over compliance:

- Instead of thinking, *"I have to keep everyone happy,"* you breathe into, *"My alignment serves everyone."*
- Instead of believing, *"I'll lose love if I tell the truth,"* you hold, *"Truth deepens real connection."*
- Instead of collapsing into, *"I need permission to choose this,"* you embody, *"My clarity is authority."*
- Instead of performing "good," you stabilize, *"Safety lives in my signal, not their approval."*

When you stabilize authenticity, the field stops reflecting conditions.

Life reorganizes around **who you are**, not who you pretend to be.

Activation

Speak this aloud:

"I release the need to perform.
I dissolve the obedience code.
I stabilize my truth.
Safety lives inside my signal."

Pause.

Place one hand on the **back of your neck** and the other on your **heart**.

Feel the back hand soften — releasing the tension of watching for external approval.

Let the body register safety **from within**.

Field in Motion

You're offered a project that looks "good" on paper — prestigious, well-paid, respected.

But your gut is screaming no.

Old programming kicks in:

"Don't burn bridges."
"You should be grateful."
"This could lead to more work."

You pause.

One hand on your heart, one at the base of your neck.

Three slow breaths.

You listen.

You decline — cleanly, simply, without over-explaining.

Within days, a new opportunity appears that feels expansive, aligned, and alive.

It was waiting for you to stop performing good and start **choosing true**.

9

DISTORTION 9: WAITING FOR THE WORLD — THE EXTERNAL PERMISSION LOOP

The External Permission Trap
You've been taught to move when the world says it's time:
- When the market is ready
- When the algorithm favors you
- When the industry shifts
- When other people "get it"

You were conditioned to believe your expansion depends on external alignment — that the field outside you must organize first before you can choose.

But waiting for the world is just another form of delay energy.

It keeps your signal paused.

And the field responds to that pause by mirroring more waiting back to you.

HOW IT HOOKS You

Waiting for the world sounds reasonable.

It sounds safe.

But underneath, the pattern is the same:

- "I'll share my work when more people understand it."
- "I'll start after the industry evolves."
- "I'll invest when the economy stabilizes."
- "I'll speak the truth when the timing is better."

Every time you hold back until the world "catches up," you're broadcasting one signal to the field:

I'm not ready.

And the field organizes around that instruction.

YOUR SIGNAL LEADS, Not Follows

The field doesn't respond to the collective timeline.

It responds to your stabilized tone.

When you broadcast readiness, reality reorders itself around you.

When you choose before permission, you stop collapsing your expansion into the pace of others.

You're not here to match the world's slowness.

You're here to set the rhythm.

REWRITING the Script

Waiting for the world dissolves when you reclaim authority over your timing:

- Instead of thinking, "I'll move when they're ready," you breathe into, **"I stabilize my readiness now."**
- Instead of believing, "I need permission to start," you hold, **"I move when my signal says move."**
- Instead of spiraling in, "I have to wait for the world to shift," you embody, **"The world organizes around my choice."**
- Instead of whispering, "Someday," you stabilize, **"I choose today."**

This isn't recklessness.

It's alignment.

You're syncing your action to your signal, not the system.

. . .

ENDING the Collective Delay

The collective is programmed to wait:
- For governments to act
- For markets to stabilize
- For people to wake up
- For conditions to be "perfect"

But perfect timing doesn't exist — there's only your timing.

The more people who stabilize now, the faster the collective reorganizes.

Your clarity leads ripple effects far beyond what you see.

ACTIVATION

Speak this aloud:
"I release the pause.
I choose before permission.
I stabilize my readiness now.
The field organizes around my broadcast."
Pause.
Place both palms lightly on your ribcage.
As you inhale, feel your ribs expand outward.
As you exhale, whisper softly: **"I move first."**
Let your body register the geometry of leading instead of waiting.

FIELD IN MOTION

You've been holding off on launching your new offer, waiting for "the right moment."
You tell yourself:
"When I have more followers."
"When the market improves."
"When the economy feels safe."
One night, clarity lands.
You pause.
Hands on ribs.

Deep breath — safe, steady, here.
You decide to move.
You post the offer without waiting for validation, certainty, or guarantees.
Within hours, the first message arrives:
Someone signs up.
Another asks for a collaboration.
A ripple begins.
It didn't happen because the world shifted first.
It happened because you did.

10

DISTORTION 10: EARNING IT — COLLAPSING THE PROVING LOOP

The Endless Proving Loop
You were programmed to believe you must earn what you want:
- Earn rest by exhausting yourself
- Earn love by being perfect
- Earn abundance by struggling for it
- Earn belonging by fitting in

This conditioning runs so deep, you might not even notice it.
It whispers in the background:
"I'll be worthy when I achieve it."
"I can receive when I've done enough."
"I'll relax once I've proven myself."
But here's the truth:
The loop never ends.
When you live inside the "earning" distortion, no milestone is ever enough — because the signal you're broadcasting is:
"I still have to prove it."
And the field mirrors that back.

. . .

WHY THE OLD Program Feels Safe

For many, the proving loop was survival:
- Families rewarded compliance and productivity
- Schools ranked your value through performance
- Jobs measured worth by output and hours
- Institutions glorified sacrifice as virtue

Your nervous system learned to equate struggle with safety.

Even when overflow knocks on the door, the body hesitates: "Did I do enough to deserve this?"

Until you rewrite this code, receiving will always feel slightly unsafe — no matter how much you "know better."

We're not debating worth here. (You were born enough.)

We're retiring the **behavior** that keeps performing for a permission slip you already hold.

THE CURRENCY of Alignment

Overflow doesn't respond to effort.

It responds to signal.
- When you stabilize safety, the field delivers more.
- When you stop performing, your capacity expands.
- When you broadcast **already**, timelines accelerate.

This is why someone working half as "hard" can experience twice the results:

Their energy isn't tangled in proving.

REWRITING the Script

Earning dissolves when you stabilize **already** as the tone of your broadcast:
- Instead of thinking, "I'll feel safe when I've done enough," you breathe into, **"Safety codes in now."**
- Instead of believing, "I have to prove I deserve this," you hold, **"My existence is the proof."**

- Instead of spiraling in, "I'll celebrate when I get there," you embody, **"I celebrate now and let overflow meet me."**
- Instead of performing, "I must earn receiving," you stabilize, **"I receive because I am."**

This isn't bypass.
It's instruction.
You're teaching your body a new way of being.

THE NERVOUS SYSTEM Reset

When you stop "earning," your biology learns a different rhythm:
- Regulated breath teaches the body that safety isn't tied to effort.
- Rest codes the system for receiving without resistance.
- Aligned action becomes intuitive, not forced.

You don't collapse timelines by doing more.
You collapse them by anchoring into **already**, now.

ACTIVATION

Speak this aloud:
"I collapse the proving loop.
I release the need to earn.
I stabilize the code of already.
Overflow meets me here."
Pause.
Rest your **forehead into your palms**, elbows on a table or your knees.
Let the weight of your head drop.
Feel gravity remind your system: you're already held. No effort required.

FIELD IN MOTION

You've been holding back from asking for help, believing you need to "handle it all yourself" to be worthy of support.

One day, you pause.
Forehead in palms.
Three deep breaths: safe, here, enough.
You reach out — simply, directly, without over-explaining.
Within an hour, a friend replies:
"Yes. I've got you."
Relief floods your body.
The field wasn't withholding support.

It was waiting for you to drop the broadcast of proving and stabilize the signal of **already**.

11

DISTORTION 11: THE WAITING ROOM — WHEN FREEZE MASQUERADES AS SAFETY

The Holding Pattern
The waiting room feels safe.
It's where you tell yourself:
- "I'll start when I'm ready."
- "I'll share when I'm confident."
- "I'll receive when I've done enough."
- "I'll leap when the timing is perfect."

But the waiting room isn't safety — it's suspension.
You're alive but not fully moving.
Breathing, but holding your breath for "later."
The longer you stay there, the more your field mirrors the same instruction back:
"Not yet. Not yet. Not yet."

WHY WE CHOOSE Delay
The waiting room is seductive because it feels protective:
- If you don't move, you can't fail
- If you don't share, you can't be judged

- If you don't leap, you can't lose
- If you don't choose, you can't choose wrong

But avoidance isn't protection — it's postponement.
You're not waiting for clarity.
You're waiting for permission you've already been given.

LIFE HAPPENS When You Move

The field doesn't respond to hesitation.
It responds to stabilization.
Hesitation broadcasts pause; one clean move ends the loop.
When you decide, the energy shifts.
When you act, timelines reorganize.
When you choose now, reality meets you here.

Every time you anchor into readiness before the evidence appears, the field catches up instantly.

It's never been about being "prepared enough."
It's about trusting the signal enough to move.

REWRITING the Script

The waiting room dissolves the moment you shift your instruction to the field:

- Instead of thinking, "I'll be ready someday," you breathe into, "**I stabilize readiness now.**"
- Instead of believing, "I'll move when I feel safe," you hold, "**I create safety by moving.**"
- Instead of spiraling in, "I need certainty first," you embody, "**My clarity arrives in motion.**"
- Instead of saying, "I'll wait for the perfect moment," you stabilize, "**This moment is the one I was waiting for.**"

This isn't about rushing.
It's about leaving the holding pattern and syncing your action to your signal.

. . .

EXITING the Loop

When you leave the waiting room:
- Energy returns to your body
- Opportunities land faster
- Decisions feel simpler and cleaner
- Overflow stabilizes without force

You realize the door was never locked.
You've been holding the handle the entire time.

ACTIVATION

Speak this aloud:
"I leave the waiting room.
I collapse the pause.
I choose myself here.
The field catches up to my movement."

Pause.

Place one hand on your **solar plexus** (just below the sternum) and the other on your **lower belly**.

Breathe deeply into your hands, feeling the expansion of your center.

Let your system register: **"I'm safe to move now."**

FIELD IN MOTION

You've been holding onto an article, waiting until it's "perfect" before publishing.

Every week, you tinker with a word, a sentence, a paragraph — but the deeper truth:

You're waiting for certainty before being seen.

One morning, you pause.

Hands resting on your center.

Three slow breaths: here, safe, now.

You post it raw.

Unfinished. Imperfect. Alive.

Within hours, someone messages you: "This landed exactly when I needed it."

It wasn't perfection that made it work.

It was leaving the waiting room.

PART II — ADVANCED MECHANICS

*uantum structure, field alignment, and the architecture of creation*

12

ESCAPE THE BINARY — LIVING BEYOND OPPOSITES

Most of the systems you grew up inside run on a single design:
Divide the field into two opposing poles and make you choose between them.
Good or bad.
Right or wrong.
Success or failure.
Spiritual or material.
The binary script trains you to reduce reality into categories, locking your signal into constant evaluation. You learn to measure yourself against someone else's definition of "enough." And when you're locked between opposites, your field gets stuck oscillating instead of expanding.

But beyond the binary lies an entirely different structure — one the field has been holding the whole time.

THE TRAP of Two-Choice Thinking

Binary programming is subtle. It feels natural because it's everywhere:

- Careers framed as safe vs. risky
- Relationships judged as right vs. wrong
- Spirituality defined as ascension vs. failure
- Productivity measured as success vs. lazy

The trap is this: when you identify with either pole, you reinforce both.

Every choice becomes an argument, and the field mirrors back conflict instead of coherence.

The signal collapses because the binary isn't real. It's a construct designed to keep you distracted from your actual power — your ability to move beyond either outcome and choose from clarity.

BEYOND OPPOSITES

The field doesn't operate in straight lines. It organizes through geometry and resonance.

From the field's perspective:

- You're not choosing between two fixed options — you're tuning into infinite available timelines.
- Every reality already exists as a frequency pattern.
- When you stabilize the signal, you unlock access to options that don't exist inside the binary framework at all.

This is the shift:

Stop negotiating between either/or.

Start embodying already/also.

STABILIZING the Third Frequency

The way out of the binary is not to choose a better pole — it's to stabilize above the polarity altogether.

Here's how:

- Catch yourself when you frame life as "this or that." Pause.
- Sense into the version of you that already lives beyond the debate.

- Choose from presence instead of defaulting to programmed roles or reactions.

When you step into the stabilized state, you're no longer bound by competing narratives.

You become the signal the field reorganizes around.

FIELD IN MOTION

You're stuck between two choices: stay where it feels safe or leap into the unknown.

Old conditioning insists:

"Pick one. Make the right move. Don't screw this up."

You pause.

You breathe.

You let your body soften and sense beyond the debate.

Then something unexpected happens — a third path appears.

One that blends what you need with what you desire.

It was invisible inside the binary, but the moment you stabilized, the geometry shifted.

Expansion didn't come from forcing a decision.

It came from stepping out of the polarity so the field could show you what was already available.

13

RECEIVING IS A SKILL — BECOMING AN OPEN SYSTEM

Most people think they have a "receiving problem." They believe they're blocked, unlucky, or "not ready." But receiving isn't magic. It isn't random. It isn't personality.

Receiving is a skill — a frequency you stabilize.

You weren't taught this. You were trained to perform for worth, earn your place, and delay your desires until some external authority declared you "deserving." But here's the truth:

The field doesn't withhold.

It circulates.

If you're not receiving, the problem isn't the field — it's the capacity you've allowed yourself to hold.

THE ARCHITECTURE of Receiving

The field operates on flow, not force.

When your system is open, energy, opportunities, relationships, and resources move toward you naturally. When it's closed, the signal gets blocked.

What closes your system:
- Believing you need to "do more" before you can receive
- Overfilling your life with noise, proving, or performance
- Distrusting the timing of what you've called in
- Resisting support because it feels uncomfortable

Receiving requires space — physically, emotionally, energetically.

You can't fill a system already overflowing with friction, obligation, or scarcity signals.

CAPACITY OVER DESERVING

You don't receive what you've earned.

You receive what you can hold.

Overflow isn't proof of worthiness — it's a reflection of capacity.

When your body, attention, and field are already saturated with unprocessed inputs, more can't stabilize, no matter how much you "deserve" it.

To open the system:
- Clear the noise that fragments attention
- Anchor into the body so the nervous system can receive
- Allow what arrives instead of second-guessing it
- Normalize overflow in small increments until it feels safe

Receiving isn't a reward.

It's alignment with the way the field already functions.

BECOMING an Open System

When you stop gripping, proving, and forcing, something shifts:
- Ideas flow through without resistance
- Support arrives without needing to chase it
- Synchronicities multiply because your tone matches availability

The more grounded your signal becomes, the more the field mirrors stability back.

Receiving is not passive — it's participatory. You create the conditions, and the field responds.

. . .

FIELD IN MOTION

You've poured yourself into a new creation. You know it's potent — alive, clean, coherent. You share it, expecting the field to light up around you.

But instead of an outpouring of feedback, you hear silence.

Old programming whispers: *"No one cares. Maybe it isn't good enough."*

But you pause. You breathe. You remember that resonance doesn't always announce itself. Some people will feel activated but stay quiet. Others will receive the signal in private. And some will resist it entirely because your coherence highlights where they're still collapsing into lack.

You didn't fail. The ripple is moving beneath the surface, reorganizing timelines you can't see yet.

So you keep creating — not for likes, comments, or validation, but because the signal is alive in you. And over time, the feedback begins to surface: a stranger reaches out saying your post changed their path. A silent reader shares how your work has been shifting their life for months.

Impact rarely moves on a visible schedule. But when you create from coherence, the field always responds.

14

MASTER THE CODES OF CREATION — DIRECTING THE FIELD

Creation isn't random.
It isn't luck. It isn't effort. It isn't chance.
Reality organizes around your stabilized frequency.
Every thought, emotion, and action sends a tone into the field. That tone becomes geometry — patterns the field reads and reflects back to you.

The question is never *"Why isn't it working?"*
The question is: *"What signal am I actually broadcasting?"*
The field doesn't respond to what you say you want.
It responds to what your system believes and stabilizes.

THE MECHANICS of the Broadcast

Your signal is built from three layers:
1 **Thoughts** — the story you tell about reality
2 **Emotions** — the frequency your body emits
3 **Actions** — how you anchor that frequency into form

When these three align, the field organizes instantly.
When they're fragmented — wanting one thing, fearing another, performing a third — the signal scrambles, and creation stalls.

The "codes of creation" are the rules of alignment. Once you understand them, you stop trying to control reality and start collaborating with it.

STABILIZING the Desired Reality

The key isn't forcing outcomes — it's stabilizing the tone of the version of you who already has what you're calling in:
- Feel it in the body first — before evidence arrives
- Speak language that reflects it as normal, not distant
- Move in coherence with the frequency, not against it
- Release timelines — the "when" collapses when the "already" is embodied

This isn't about pretending.
It's about tuning.
You become the version of you who already holds the thing (because you do) — and the field mirrors that back.

STOP TRYING to Control the Field

Control is scarcity disguised as strategy.
It creates resistance, delays timelines, and scrambles the signal.
The shift is subtle but profound:
- Forcing says: *"I need this to happen so I can feel okay."*
- Directing says: *"I stabilize the tone where this already exists, and I allow the field to organize naturally."*

The less you chase, the faster the alignment locks in.

THE ART of Non-Attachment

Non-attachment doesn't mean detachment.
It means your identity isn't tied to the outcome.
You've stabilized the frequency of overflow so deeply that the result becomes inevitable — but you aren't gripping it.
Paradoxically, this is the moment creation accelerates:

The signal becomes clean, the field responds, and timelines collapse around coherence. But remember the field may also reflect something back that you did not expect. It knows what you need.

FIELD IN MOTION

You've been trying to call in a new home for months.

You've made vision boards, scrolled endlessly, and obsessively checked listings, but nothing aligns.

One night, you sit quietly and tune into the version of you who already lives in the space you want.

You feel the light on your face, the quiet in the room, the sense of already here.

Within a week, a listing appears you hadn't seen before. The price works. The timing works. Everything clicks into place.

You didn't force it.

You stabilized the tone, and the field reflected the match.

15

REWRITE THE IDENTITY GRID — STABILIZING WHO YOU ARE

Your reality is organized around an invisible framework: your identity grid.
Every belief you hold about who you are — spoken or unspoken — broadcasts a frequency into the field. That frequency
informs what's possible, what's allowed, and what repeats.
If your identity says *"I'm always behind,"* the field matches it.
If your identity says *"I have to work twice as hard,"* you'll keep attracting struggle.
If your identity says *"I'm unworthy,"* you'll meet timelines that mirror that back.
But identity isn't truth.
It's a program — one you can rewrite.

HOW THE GRID (The Overlay) Gets Built
Your identity formed long before you chose it.
It was constructed from:
- Family systems — rules about belonging, love, and "how we survive"

- Cultural scripts — who you should be to be accepted
- Personal narratives — meanings you assigned to failure, rejection, or success
- Collective programming — the inherited illusions of scarcity, worth, and separation

Over time, these beliefs wove together into a grid — a network of assumptions about *"who I am"* and *"how life works."*

But when the grid runs on distortion, the field reflects distortion back.

UPGRADING the Signal

The key to rewriting identity isn't force — it's stabilization.

Instead of fighting the old stories, you shift your broadcast by embodying the version of you who already lives the reality you want.

- Catch the identities running in the background: *"I'm not ready," "I'm not enough," "I'm always struggling."*
- Sense into the self that exists beyond them — the one not coded by proving or scarcity.
- Speak and act from that stabilized tone, even before evidence arrives.

When your identity grid upgrades, your entire field reorganizes. The timelines available to you shift instantly.

LIVING FROM COHERENCE

Rewriting the identity grid isn't just about changing beliefs — it's about living from truth.

Truth *is* coherence. It's the alignment between what you know, what you feel, what you choose, and what you broadcast into the field.

When your identity is built from distortion, you leak energy trying to **perform** a version of yourself that isn't real. But when you stabilize in truth, your nervous system relaxes, your choices become cleaner, and your signal strengthens.

Living from coherence means:

- You no longer act from proving or fear — your actions are anchored in clarity
- You stop outsourcing your worth to roles, labels, and expectations
- You broadcast from the version of you that already exists beyond performance

Coherence collapses delay because the field can finally trust your signal.

When your inner tone matches your outer expression, reality organizes faster and cleaner — not because you "did more," but because you stopped splitting your energy between who you are and who you *think* you need to be.

IDENTITY VS. AUTHENTICITY

Identity can become a trap if it's built from performance.

You curate, control, and edit yourself to match a role — *"good parent," "successful entrepreneur," "spiritual seeker."*

But coherence requires authenticity:

- Drop the identities you've outgrown
- Stop performing for safety or belonging
- Let yourself become the signal, not the mask

You're not here to reinforce a role.

You're here to embody resonance.

REWRITING the Grid in Real Time

Rebuilding the identity grid is an ongoing practice:

- Pause before defaulting to the old version of you
- Choose language that aligns with the new frequency
- Make micro-decisions from the upgraded signal until it normalizes

in your nervous system
This isn't about inventing a "better" self.
It's about removing distortion until only your original signal remains.

FIELD IN MOTION

You've been saying for years, *"I'm terrible with money."*
It's a casual line, but the field takes it literally — reflecting scarcity timelines back again and again.
One day, you decide to change the signal.
You stop speaking that identity into existence.
You begin tracking your spending, stabilizing your body while receiving, and speaking overflow as normal.
A few weeks later, an unexpected payment arrives.
It's not coincidence — it's geometry.
The moment you rewrote the identity grid, the field updated to match.

16

THE BODY BROADCAST — NERVOUS SYSTEM AS FIELD TECHNOLOGY

Your nervous system is not separate from your abundance.
It is the transmitter.
The regulator.
The live interface between the tone you *think* you're sending...
and the tone the field actually receives.
The field does not decode your affirmations.
It decodes your state.
It listens to the geometry of your fascia, the rhythm of your breath, the openness of your tissues.
Every "manifestation delay" is not a failure of effort —
but a mirror of what your body is stabilized to hold.

WHEN YOU ARE DYSREGULATED:
- Signal static increases
- Nervous system tightens
- Perception contracts
- Scarcity loops feel "real"
- Urgency hijacks precision
- Timelines stretch and slow

- Manifestation becomes distorted or delayed

The field reflects confusion.

WHEN YOU ARE REGULATED:
- Signal becomes clear
- Breath stabilizes presence
- Capacity expands
- Perception widens
- Coherence holds in real time
- Timelines collapse
- Reality organizes with elegance and speed

The field reflects clarity.

RECODING THE BODY

You don't manifest what you think.
You manifest what your nervous system has made *safe*.
And safety is not an idea — it is a **physiological frequency**.
Breath is not spiritual fluff.
It is signal stabilization.
It is timeline compression.
This isn't about "doing more."
It's about transmitting from within your actual capacity.
Your body is not in the way.
It is the way.

FIELD IN MOTION

You've been working on your mindset, saying the right words, visualizing the future.
But nothing moves.
Because inside, your system is still broadcasting urgency.
One morning, you stop.
You breathe.

You let your body fully land — no proving, no striving.
You feel everything in the silence.
You stabilize.
That week, timelines collapse:
A stalled project completes.
A partner opens up.
A long-delayed payment lands.
It wasn't your thoughts that shifted it.
It was your signal — finally coherent enough to hold it.

17

YOUR BODY IS THE ANTENNA

Your body isn't separate from your signal. It is the signal's translator. Every field broadcast begins in your biology. Your fascia, tissues, and nervous system don't just respond to energy—they transmit it. The body is the real-time antenna between internal frequency and external reality.

THE BODY AS TRANSLATOR

What you call intuition, clarity, or resonance isn't conceptual. It's somatic. Your system is wired to read geometry:

- Fascia acts like fiber-optic cable, transmitting sensation and signal instantly
- Your gut and heart contain neural networks that decode subtle field shifts before your mind can
- Your posture, breath, and tone reveal your current signal more honestly than any thought

This is why the body never lies. You might say, "I'm open," but if your jaw is clenched and your chest is tight, the field hears contraction.

. . .

COHERENCE IS A PHYSICAL FREQUENCY

To stabilize overflow, your tissues must normalize expansion. Otherwise, your body will keep reverting to safety patterns: bracing, shrinking, armoring. These patterns aren't flaws—they're outdated coding.

To shift the signal, you update the hardware:
- Breathe in rhythms that calm your nervous system
- Stretch and soften the fascia so signal flows freely
- Move and orient your body in ways that tell the field: I'm available

BODY-BASED INTUITION True intuition doesn't yell. It signals through:
- A subtle pull toward something
- A relaxation in the system
- A quickening or expansion in the heart or gut

When you're regulated, you can hear it. When you're dysregulated, intuition gets distorted by urgency or fear.

This is why regulating the body is the gateway to clearer guidance. It's not about "getting answers." It's about becoming the space that can receive them.

FIELD IN MOTION

You're debating a decision that looks logical on paper, but your body tightens every time you speak it aloud. Instead of overriding it, you pause. You place a hand on your gut, breathe deeply, and wait.

A few hours later, a completely different opportunity shows up—one that makes your whole body exhale. You didn't "think" your way there. You listened to your antenna.

18

THE PHYSICS OF YOU

You are not a fixed identity. You are a waveform. Your system is not built for hustle, forcing, or mental override. It's built for frequency-based creation. Everything you broadcast becomes geometry. Every tone you stabilize becomes structure.

This is not metaphysics. It's mechanics.

YOU ARE A BIOELECTRIC FIELD

Every cell in your body emits an electromagnetic signal. Your heart field extends several feet beyond your skin. Your fascia conducts charge. Your nervous system is a pattern-recognition tool that constantly adjusts to internal and external stimuli.

When you change your breath, you shift your charge. When you regulate your state, you realign the signal. This is why manifestation isn't magic. It's energetic architecture.

RESIDENCY VS. REPETITION

Creating reality isn't about repeating mantras or forcing positive thoughts. It's about **residency**:

- Can your system hold the frequency of what you say you want?
- Can you breathe while holding it?
- Can you stay in that tone when there's no evidence yet?

Reality doesn't respond to what you *visit*. It responds to what you *live in*.

COHERENCE COLLAPSES TIME

When your signal is clean—body, breath, tone aligned—timelines collapse. Why? Because there's no contradiction for the field to resolve. No resistance to navigate. No distortion to delay.

Coherence doesn't guarantee instant outcomes. But it does guarantee one thing: you'll stop leaking energy. You'll stop scrambling the geometry. And reality will organize with speed and elegance.

FIELD IN MOTION

You're used to over-explaining, over-efforting, overthink-ing. But this time, you just breathe. You choose stillness. You let your body speak first.

Instead of pitching or chasing, you embody. Instead of trying to convince the field, you broadcast from clarity.

And without pushing, it lands. Because physics always reflects frequency.

19
INTEGRATION INSTABILITY — THE OSCILLATION BETWEEN WHO YOU WERE AND WHO YOU ARE BECOMING

There is a moment in the coherence journey that few name, yet most endure. It is the in-between: the space where the old self has collapsed, but the new signal has not fully stabilized.

This chapter names that space.

Integration Instability is not regression. It is the oscillation between two operating systems—the conditioned identity built for survival, and the emergent architecture aligned with truth.

It is not a sign that you are failing. It is a sign that the field is rewiring.

What Is Integration Instability?

It is the energetic whiplash between clarity and confusion. Peace and panic. Trust and terror. Presence and pattern.

You are no longer in full resonance with the old world—its demands, distortions, and frequency contracts. But you are not yet fully fluent in the new one.

And so you oscillate.

This is not dysfunction. This is *coherence recalibration*.

Every time you return to your breath, even amidst doubt, you are proving signal memory. Every time you fall back into loops, but notice faster, you are accelerating field awareness.

This is the bridge phase. Not everyone makes it through.

Why It Happens

Your nervous system was trained to anchor to fear, over-efforting, control, and mental dominance.

As you begin to anchor in breath, stillness, presence, and trust, those systems lose their grip—but they don't disappear quietly. They flare. They spike. They scream.

Your system interprets this as failure. It is not.

It is death-throes of an obsolete pattern.

You are exiting performance. You are exiting the survival-based economy of self-worth.

But without the old metrics (effort, achievement, validation), your identity destabilizes.

Until it doesn't.

Loop Mechanics

The Integration Instability Loop looks like this:
- Clarity. Trust. Peace.
- Spike. Doubt. Fear.
- Collapse. Control. Withdrawal.
- Breath. Presence. Reset.
- Repeat.

This loop is *not regression*. It is a **signal-clearing spiral**. Each rotation moves faster. The return to coherence gets quicker.

Your nervous system is learning how to stabilize under the frequency of truth. That is *not* an instant switch. It is a biological and electromagnetic evolution.

. . .

How To Navigate It

1 Remove "Am I doing this right?" from your vocabulary. That question comes from the external reward system. It has no place in coherence.

"Am I doing it right?"

Replace with:

"Am I fully here right now?"

That is the only metric that matters.

2 Use breath as presence, not as a fix. You are not breathing to calm down. You are breathing to stabilize your signal.

3 Do not label the wave. If sadness comes, let it. If numbness comes, let it. If fear comes, *feel* it. But do not narrate it.

4 Protect your field. Do not broadcast into distorted spaces during instability. You will interpret rejection as personal rather than energetic.

5 Anchor through embodiment. Move. Walk. Stretch. Touch the earth. Stability is not found in thought—only in sensation.

Try This: 3 breaths. 1 sentence: "I am fully here." Feel. Wait. Witness. Nothing to fix.

Micro-Triggers to Watch For:
- Checking your bank balance and feeling contraction.
- Scrolling social media and entering comparison collapse.
- Doing nothing and feeling guilty.
- Expressing truth and then questioning if it was "too much."

Each of these moments is not failure. It is the field recalibrating. Pause. Breathe. Stay.

What Stabilizes Over Time

Eventually, the old loops dissolve. They stop flaring. They lose charge. They become echoes instead of triggers.

Your system begins to trust:
- Silence.
- Unknowns.
- Ease.

- Receiving.
- Self-guided action without permission or proof.

You begin to live from the inside out. That is when wealth, love, expression, and visibility become effortless. Not because you chased them—but because you stabilized the signal they flow through.

This is the passage through the threshold.

You are not unstable. You are unlearning distortion.

You are not broken. You are integrating your original architecture.

You are not behind. You are *in process*.

Hold the line. Breathe through the static. The field is recalibrating.

THE FIELD IN MOTION

Oscillation is not collapse. It is motion through distortion.

Every return to breath is a recalibration. Every moment of presence is signal stabilization.

The field is not asking for perfection. It is asking you to stay. To feel. To trust coherence even when the evidence isn't instant.

This is the motion of remembrance. This is the return.

And in time, this inner stability becomes the only flow you trust.

20

TRUSTING THE FLOW — PRECISION WITHOUT FORCE

Control is a trauma response disguised as strategy.
It tells you:
"If I manage everything perfectly, I'll be safe."
But control is static in the field — it signals fear, not coherence.
True creation isn't about gripping tighter.
It's about trusting the flow: allowing the field to organize in alignment
with your stabilized tone while you stay grounded in clear, intentional action.
Flow is not passive.
It's precision without force.

THE MECHANICS of Resistance
Resistance happens when your identity, desires, and actions aren't aligned.
- You want expansion, but your nervous system broadcasts fear.
- You want overflow, but your identity says you're "not ready."
- You force timelines from scarcity, creating more delay.

This fragmentation scrambles the signal.

Instead of magnetizing, you repel.
Instead of receiving, you chase.
The field reads clarity, not effort.
Until you stabilize trust, force keeps creating friction.

THE ARCHITECTURE of Flow

Flow doesn't mean "do nothing."
It means moving in rhythm with the geometry of the field:
- **Listen:** tune into the subtle pulls of your own body's intelligence.
- **Align:** choose actions that match the signal you've already stabilized.
- **Release:** let go of timelines and outcomes the moment you broadcast the tone.

When your nervous system is regulated and your actions are coherent, momentum compounds naturally.

The field doesn't need micromanagement — it responds to stability.

PRECISION WITHOUT FORCE

Most people mistake control for clarity.
But clarity comes from signal, not strategy.
- Control grips because it doesn't trust the field.
- Force drains energy because it moves against resonance.
- Precision chooses aligned action, then lets the geometry unfold.

This isn't "blind faith."
It's a knowing: the field is always moving in response to your broadcast.
Trusting flow accelerates creation because resistance isn't blocking the signal.

RECLAIMING TRUST

Trust isn't something you perform — it's something you stabilize.
- Notice when urgency rises: breathe into presence before acting
- Question where you're forcing outcomes instead of allowing them
- Anchor into the feeling of *"already here"* before the evidence appears
- Act from clarity, not panic

The more you regulate trust in your system, the more naturally timelines collapse around you.

FIELD IN MOTION

You've been pushing and striving — sending endless messages, forcing timelines, trying to make something click.

Finally, you pause.

You breathe. You feel the tension in your body and let it soften.

From that regulated space, you choose one simple, aligned action — a message, a phone call, a quiet decision you've been avoiding.

You take the step and release the outcome completely.

Two days later, the response comes — not because you hustled harder, but because you stopped scrambling your signal.

By stabilizing trust and acting from coherence, you opened the geometry for the right pieces to land without force.

21

CREATIVE SOVEREIGNTY — EXPRESSING FROM YOUR OVERFLOW

Your creativity isn't separate from the field.
It **is** the field, moving through you.
But for most people, expression gets hijacked early:
- You learn to create for approval instead of resonance
- You perform for belonging instead of transmitting truth
- You hold back ideas because they don't fit the "market"
- You measure your value by how others respond

This distortion fractures your signal.

When creativity becomes a performance, you disconnect from the source it flows from.

Creative sovereignty returns you to alignment:

You express, not to prove — but to participate in the field's natural expansion.

THE GEOMETRY of Overflow

Creation multiplies when you stop trying to own it.

You're not generating from nothing; you're tuning into existing currents in the field and translating them into form.

Overflow happens when:

- You've stabilized your signal so deeply that expression feels inevitable
- You release timelines, outcomes, and "success metrics"
- You create without making your identity dependent on the result

This is why creativity feels effortless when your field is coherent: you're no longer chasing permission, you're broadcasting truth.

THE TRAP of Performed Creativity

When you create from distortion, the work gets heavy:
- You filter your ideas to be acceptable
- You sacrifice authenticity to appease algorithms or audiences
- You treat expression like labor instead of translation

But creative sovereignty dissolves the middleman.

The field already carries infinite inspiration — you stop searching,

and you start receiving.

Expression becomes direct transmission.

Unforced. Alive. Magnetic.

LIVING as the Signal

When you stabilize creative sovereignty, your work no longer defines your worth.

You're not seeking relevance. **You are resonance.**
- You create because it wants to move
- You trust the forms it takes without over-editing them to "fit"
- You follow what lights up your system instead of bending to external standards

This is how your creations ripple: they're born from truth, not performance.

And truth carries its own gravity.

. . .

CREATIVE SOVEREIGNTY in Practice
- Begin with overflow, not scarcity. Fill your system before creating.
- Let go of perfectionism — coherence lands more powerfully than polish.
- Stop pre-deciding how your work "should" be received.
- Follow what excites you now instead of predicting what will "sell later."

The clearer your signal, the more naturally your creations find their place in the field.

FIELD IN MOTION

You've been agonizing over a launch, trying to make it "perfect" before sharing it.

Every time you edit it for what you think people want, the energy drains out.

Finally, you decide to strip it back to its core — the message you actually believe.

You share it as-is, no filters, no manipulation, no performance.

Within hours, the responses come in.

People feel it because it's real.

You didn't push harder — you broadcasted cleanly.

PART III — EMBODIMENT & OVERFLOW

P*ractical, embodied integration for stabilizing coherence in daily life*

22

BUILD THE CONTAINER — HOLDING MORE WITHOUT LEAKS

Abundance doesn't just flow **in** — it flows **through**.
If your system isn't built to **hold** what's arriving, it slips away as quickly as it comes.

A **container** is anything — physical, energetic, emotional, or structural — that creates the stability for **energy, money, opportunities, relationships, and creative flow** to land, integrate, and **multiply**.

Without containers, your field scatters.

With them, overflow stabilizes.

This isn't about discipline for discipline's sake.

It's about **coherence** — building frameworks that **support expansion** instead of sabotaging it.

Overflow isn't a moment. It's a **capacity**.

Your container determines how much of it you can sustain.

WHY MOST CONTAINERS LEAK

You've been taught to "manifest more," but rarely taught how to **hold** it.

Energy, money, and opportunities flow to the **level of structure** your system can stabilize.

Leaks often show up as:
- Unfinished commitments draining attention
- Unclear boundaries scattering energy
- Physical clutter mirroring mental static
- Emotional loops that haven't been resolved
- Overfilling your calendar with misaligned obligations

Leaky containers create chaotic fields. No matter how powerful your signal is, energy won't stabilize if it has nowhere to **land**.

EXAMPLES OF CONTAINERS

Here's what containers actually look like in real life:

Financial Containers — *holding money*
- A clear system for where your income flows: bills, savings, overflow, play
- Separate accounts so money has "homes" instead of bleeding everywhere
- Tracking inflows and outflows so your nervous system normalizes holding more

Without a container: You get a big payment, it feels chaotic, and the money disappears.

With a container: Your body trusts what's arriving, and the field mirrors that stability with more.

Time Containers — *holding presence*
- Creating intentional blocks for deep work instead of reacting all day
- Building white space into your schedule to avoid overfilling capacity
- Setting start-and-stop boundaries to prevent energy leaks

Without a container: You're scattered, overbooked, and depleted.

With a container: You have energy to **create** instead of constantly managing chaos.

CREATIVE CONTAINERS — *holding ideas*
- Setting aside structured time to focus on one project without multitasking
- Choosing **one** primary outlet instead of splitting energy across five
- Keeping an "idea dropbox" or system for capturing inspiration so nothing gets lost

Without a container: Creative sparks dissolve into overwhelm.

With a container: Energy compounds, projects finish, and momentum stabilizes.

ENERGETIC CONTAINERS — *holding your signal*
- Breathwork, grounding, and nervous system regulation so your body codes safety
- Rituals that reset your frequency after interactions, work, or social media
- Tuning into what your field actually wants before reacting to outside noise

Without a container: Other people's energy floods your system.

With a container: You broadcast from clarity and magnetize opportunities that match your signal.

RELATIONSHIP CONTAINERS — *holding connection*
- Setting clear expectations and agreements with partners, clients, or collaborators
- Naming your boundaries instead of silently resenting
- Choosing who gets access to your energy based on coherence, not obligation

Without a container: Relationships drain your field.

With a container: Relationships **amplify** your signal instead of collapsing it.

BUILDING STRUCTURES THAT SUPPORT FLOW

A healthy container creates clarity, stability, and trust within your system. Start small, then build gradually:

- Simplify your space: Clear physical environments signal readiness to the field
- Clarify your yes/no: Boundaries protect your energy and prevent collapse
- Close open loops: Finish unresolved tasks or consciously release them
- Create systems that breathe: Avoid rigidity; leave space for intuition and integration

Your structure should **expand your signal**, not trap it. It's not about perfection — it's about alignment.

CAPACITY IS SAFETY

Your nervous system decides how much overflow you can hold. If receiving more feels unsafe, your body will unconsciously reject it.

To build capacity:

- Regulate through breath and grounding practices
- Normalize small increments of overflow before stretching further
- Anchor new realities in your senses — see them, feel them, embody them
- Let your body know it's safe to hold **more than before**

The stronger your container, the safer your system feels — and the more naturally the field mirrors that stability.

FIELD IN MOTION

You receive an unexpected amount of money — more than you're used to holding.

The old pattern kicks in: "Spend it fast before it disappears."

This time, you pause. You set up a simple structure: a small savings jar, a playful fund, a space for generosity.

A month later, something new clicks: the money's still here, your body feels calmer holding it, and more has arrived.

Overflow isn't just receiving more.

It's learning to hold what you've already called in — and letting the field mirror your stability.

23

THE BODY REMEMBERS — EXPANDING CAPACITY THROUGH PRESENCE

You can't think your way out of chaos.
You can't exit survival loops through knowledge.
Because loops don't live in the mind.
They live in the **body** — inside your nervous system, where your patterns of safety, expansion, and contraction are coded.

This is why "knowing better" rarely changes anything. You've read the books, you've had the insights, you've seen the mechanics — and still, sometimes, nothing shifts.

It isn't because you're broken. It's because your **nervous system** doesn't yet *believe* you're safe in a new reality.

Your body will always choose the **familiar** over the **possible** — even if what's familiar keeps you looping in scarcity, overworking, self-abandonment, or fear. The nervous system is wired for survival, not expansion. If "too much" feels foreign, the system shuts it down.

Overflow doesn't stabilize in the mind first.
It stabilizes in the body.

Why Safety Unlocks **Abundance**

The field mirrors what your body can hold. When your nervous system broadcasts threat, chaos, or fear, the geometry collapses timelines into self-protection. You unconsciously reject the very realities you're calling in — not because you don't deserve them, but because your system can't **receive** what it doesn't trust.

This is why you see the same loops playing out:
- Saying yes when you mean no
- Gripping timelines out of fear of loss
- Avoiding visibility because being seen feels dangerous
- Calling in opportunities you then can't sustain

It isn't willpower that breaks the cycle.

It's **capacity**.

Your capacity expands when your body learns a new baseline of safety — when "overflow" stops feeling like threat and starts feeling normal.

BREATH as the Reset Point

Breath is the fastest way to collapse distortion because it bypasses thought entirely. It moves signal directly through the body, teaching your nervous system safety **in real time.**

- Shallow, fast breaths code the body for danger → the field mirrors urgency and contraction.
- Slow, deep, rhythmic breathing codes safety → the field mirrors coherence and stability.

Each time you pause and breathe, you're not "calming down." You're **reprogramming your baseline.** You're teaching the body to hold more without spiraling into fight, flight, or freeze.

Breath isn't optional for overflow.

It's the gateway.

SOMATIC EXPANSION: Making Space Inside

When life feels chaotic, it's rarely because "too much" is happening. It's because there's **not enough space** inside you to hold what's arriving.

Somatic expansion is the practice of deliberately creating more space within your body so your field can stabilize. It's simple:

1 Pause. Close your eyes.
2 Feel where tension is stored — chest, belly, jaw, shoulders.
3 Breathe into that exact point, imagining your body softening around it.
4 Widen your awareness. Sense the edges of your body expanding, like you're growing a bigger container for energy to move through.

With practice, your system learns: **it's safe to hold more.**
And the field mirrors that new signal instantly.

Integration Practices

You don't have to force change. You allow it by teaching the body safety, over and over. Start small:

- **Micro-breath resets:** Take three deep belly breaths whenever you notice contraction.
- **Grounding awareness:** Place your feet on the floor and name five things you can physically feel. This signals safety to the body instantly.
- **Release through movement:** Shaking, stretching, dancing, walking barefoot — anything that lets stuck energy move through you.
- **Stillness:** Simply sit, breathe, and listen. Presence collapses loops faster than force ever could.

Activation

*"I exit the loop of urgency.
I stabilize safety in my body.
I allow my nervous system to expand its capacity to hold more.
I breathe presence into my signal.
I let the field organize around my coherence."*

. . .

FIELD IN MOTION

You're feeling overwhelmed — your inbox is full, bills are due, your mind is spinning.

Old programming says: "Push harder. Fix it faster."

Instead, you pause. You breathe — deep, slow, grounded. You place your hand on your chest and feel your body soften beneath it.

Five minutes later, something shifts. The chaos feels less urgent. Clarity returns. You handle what's needed without spiraling.

You didn't "manifest" calm.

You created safety, and the field reorganized around it.

24

MONEY LOVES CLARITY — CLEANING THE SIGNAL OF EXCHANGE

Money is energy in motion.
It's not moral. It's not emotional. It's not personal.
It's a mirror.

Money flows where your signal is clean. It slows, leaks, or bypasses when distortion takes over. If your relationship with money is loaded with guilt, fear, avoidance, or proving, the field reflects that back:

- Opportunities stall
- Payments delay
- Overflow spikes and disappears instead of stabilizing

Money isn't the block.
Distortion is.

THE FREQUENCY OF EXCHANGE

Money is circulation — it amplifies whatever's happening in your field:

- When you stabilize overflow, it multiplies.
- When you stabilize scarcity, it contracts.
- When your signal is scrambled, it mirrors chaos.

This is why no strategy, budget, or spreadsheet can override a distorted broadcast.

Money responds to coherence, not control.

To shift your relationship with it, you don't manage harder — you clarify deeper.

MONEY AS RELATIONSHIP

Money isn't neutral numbers on a spreadsheet.

It's a living relationship — one that responds to the signals you hold and the stories you carry.

Like any relationship, money thrives on respect and communication:

- Ignoring it creates distrust and instability.
- Clinging to it signals fear and blocks flow.
- Using it performatively fractures your connection with overflow.
- Meeting it openly codes safety into the field.

When you stabilize trust, your entire financial reality reorganizes.

RELEASING OLD MONEY STORIES

Most money distortions aren't yours.

They're inherited programs running beneath awareness:

- "I have to work harder than everyone else to deserve it."
- "People with money are greedy."
- "I can't hold onto it, so why try?"
- "I'll feel safe when I finally have enough."

These scripts broadcast static into the field, recreating limitation even when you're "doing everything right."

The moment you rewrite the story, the broadcast shifts.

CLEANING THE SIGNAL

Money loves precision, openness, and neutrality. Start here:

- **Get honest** — Know exactly where money is moving, without spiraling into shame.
- **Stop avoiding** — Clarity dissolves fear. Open the statements you've been ignoring.
- **Detach worth from numbers** — Your balance is feedback, not identity.
- **Circulate consciously** — Spend and share from alignment, not panic or performance.

When you stop hiding from money, money stops hiding from you.

RELEASING THE PERFORMANCE LOOP

Many people perform "abundance" to look successful — buying things to project an image, saying yes to obligations to seem generous, or overspending for validation.

But performance drains more than it multiplies.

True overflow doesn't need to prove anything.

It feels neutral. Alive. Effortless.

When your money choices come from alignment instead of proving, circulation becomes natural again.

THE FIELD LOVES TRANSPARENCY

The clearer your signal, the cleaner your magnetism:
- Define your standards for receiving.
- Ask for what you want without apology.
- Treat money as an ally, not a judge.
- Give without leaking, and receive without collapsing.

Money loves clarity because clarity stabilizes trust — and trust opens flow.

PRACTICES FOR BUILDING TRUST

- Create intentional check-ins, not reactive panic sessions.

- Release guilt-based spending and replace it with conscious circulation.
- Speak about money clearly and neutrally — without apology.
- Anchor gratitude before, during, and after exchange.

Safety codes overflow. When your system trusts itself, the field mirrors it back.

CORE TRANSMISSION

Money isn't your source.

You are.

The field doesn't respond to how hard you hustle or how well you strategize.

It responds to the clarity you stabilize, the stories you dissolve, and the safety your body can hold.

Money loves clarity because clarity signals trust.

Trust opens flow.

FIELD IN MOTION

You've been avoiding your bank account because it triggers anxiety.

One morning, you decide to face it. You open everything, organize your numbers, and breathe through the discomfort.

You set up a simple structure — assigning percentages and creating space for overflow. Two days later, a delayed payment clears.

The moment you stopped hiding, money stopped hiding too.

25

TIME IS WEALTH — RECLAIMING CYCLICAL FLOW

You were taught that time is scarce.
That it slips away, that there's never enough, that you're always "behind."
This distortion turns your life into a race against the clock, creating urgency loops that scramble your field.
But time isn't linear — that's a human overlay.
In the field, time behaves differently.
It bends, stretches, and reorganizes itself around stabilized frequency.
When you treat time as wealth, you step out of survival pace and into coherent flow.
You stop chasing hours and start expanding moments.

LINEAR TIME vs. Cyclical Flow

The belief that time is fixed forces you into scarcity:
- You over-schedule, overcommit, and burn out trying to "keep up"
- You collapse your nervous system into urgency and reactivity
- You choose speed over alignment and force over presence

But time is not a straight line — it's geometric.

The more coherent your broadcast, the more fluidly timelines reorganize around you.

This is why a single aligned hour can produce more than an entire week of forced effort.

REDEFINING Wealth

Wealth isn't just stored in numbers — it's stored in your capacity to be present.

- When you rush, you disconnect from the field
- When you slow down intentionally, you amplify precision
- When you stabilize now, you access possibilities unavailable in urgency

True abundance expands through spaciousness.

You create more wealth by reclaiming your time, not trading more of it away.

CREATING Coherent Rhythms

Reclaiming time means restructuring how energy moves through your system:

- **Simplify your commitments:** Reduce noise to make space for clarity
- **Anchor presence practices:** Breath, body awareness, and micro-pauses reset your field
- **Work with your peaks:** Align effort with your natural cycles of energy, not external demands
- **Create intentional spaciousness:** Time isn't managed; it's magnetized

The more aligned your rhythms become, the more magnetic your field feels.

Spaciousness accelerates timelines.

. . .

YOUR BODY as a Clock

Your nervous system determines how you experience time.
When you're fragmented, moments feel rushed and chaotic.
When you're regulated, time expands.
Learning to access coherence through the body collapses delay:
- Slow your breath to stabilize presence
- Reset posture to ground into clarity
- Sense into the timeline where what you want already exists

When the body relaxes, the field organizes faster.

FIELD IN MOTION

You've been buried under back-to-back tasks, convinced there's no room to breathe.

Finally, you step outside, pause, and take five deep breaths.

The tension doesn't release right away — but over the next few hours, your body softens, and your clarity begins returning.

That evening, an idea surfaces naturally, showing you the simplest path forward.

When you step out of urgency, the timelines open — sometimes subtly, sometimes slowly, but always in motion.

26

EXPRESSION MULTIPLIES — MOVING TRUTH THROUGH YOU

Expression is expansion.
Every time you allow truth to move through you — through words, art, presence, or action — you amplify your signal and open new timelines.

But for most people, expression gets trapped inside distortion:
- You overthink instead of translating what's alive right now
- You censor yourself to fit the "right" audience or narrative
- You create from proving instead of transmitting resonance
- You equate expression with outcomes, expecting it to deliver validation

When expression is bound to performance, it contracts your field. When expression is free, it multiplies energy, coherence, and connection.

THE GEOMETRY of Transmission

Expression isn't about forcing impact — it's about becoming a clear channel for what wants to move:
- Thoughts arise, energy flows, and you let it translate without

gripping the result
- Your frequency leads, and form follows naturally
- The less you interfere, the purer the transmission

This is why some expressions land so deeply: they're coded with coherence, not manipulation.

When your body, mind, and signal align, the field mirrors back amplified flow.

CLEARING EXPRESSION DISTORTION

Expression contracts when it's entangled with fear or control:
- Holding back truths to avoid conflict
- Over-explaining to manage perception
- Polishing ideas endlessly instead of sharing them alive
- Comparing your output to others and collapsing into doubt

These distortions freeze the very energy meant to move through you.

Expression isn't about perfecting the form — it's about staying in motion.

EXPRESSION AS CIRCULATION

Truth flows like breath. When you withhold it, you stagnate. When you let it move, you open channels for more to arrive:
- Ideas compound when you release them
- Opportunities flow where your voice creates clarity
- Relationships deepen when you bring your authentic self forward

Expression doesn't drain your field when it comes from coherence

— it replenishes it.

PRACTICES FOR AMPLIFYING Expression
- Stop editing your voice to be palatable or strategic

- Share what's alive in real-time instead of waiting for perfect form
- Follow the creative impulse when it arises — don't outsource its timing
- Treat your body as an instrument of translation: sound, movement, writing, and presence all carry your signal

The more freely truth moves through you, the more naturally abundance multiplies around you.

FIELD IN MOTION

You've been sitting on an idea, unsure if anyone will "get it."

One morning, you write the post exactly as it came — no edits, no performing.

The first day, it lands quietly.

Days later, the energy begins to circulate — a small handful of deep comments, then a DM from someone who's been silently following your work for months.

Not every signal is loud when it first moves — but expression always multiplies beneath the surface.

27

SPEAK WHAT YOU WANT — CODING THE FIELD THROUGH LANGUAGE

Language doesn't just describe reality, it directs it.
Words aren't neutral.
They code the field.
Every sentence you speak sends a frequency into motion — either reinforcing a past loop or building a new geometry for reality to organize around.

But here's the part most teachings skip:
Your words only hold power when your body can back them.
You can say "I'm abundant" a thousand times, but if your breath is tight and your nervous system is bracing, the field won't hear the words.
It will hear the static.

BREATH IS THE CALIBRATION TOOL

Breath calibrates your tone.
Presence infuses your signal with clarity.
Language becomes directive when your entire system — body, breath, tone, field — says the same thing.
This is why affirmations often fail.

They come from the mouth, but not the body.
They override instead of stabilize.
They try to convince the field, rather than instruct it.
But when your language emerges from a regulated system:
- Your tone carries authority without force
- Your words feel clean, clear, and non-performative
- The field reflects quickly because there's no static to decode

THE 3-LAYER BROADCAST: BODY. BREATH. WORD.

1 **BODY** — Your nervous system is either in contraction or coherence. Your tissues tell the field what you can hold.

2 **BREATH** — Your breath tells the field whether you're present or pretending.

3 **WORD** — Your language seals the code. It clarifies the geometry you're stabilizing.

When all three align, words don't perform. They program.

COMMON WAYS SIGNALS GET SCRAMBLED
- Speaking from fear: "I hope this works out" — while your body says "I don't believe it"
- Softening truth to avoid discomfort: "It's fine, I'm okay" — when you're not
- Complaining, venting, gossiping — repetition of frequencies you're trying to leave

These aren't moral issues.
They're mechanics.
What you say, stabilized through what you feel, codes what you live.

NEW LANGUAGE PRACTICE
- Say what you want, not what you fear.

- Use present tense: "This is stabilizing" instead of "Someday it might."
- Replace softening fillers with signal statements: "I am available for that. I am not available for that."

FIELD IN MOTION

You're catching up with a friend who asks, "How's life feeling lately?"
The old impulse rises — to vent, minimize, or default to autopilot.
Instead, you pause.
You breathe.
You feel your feet on the ground.
You say:
"I'm feeling more at home in myself than ever."
A few days later, you're invited to something that feels like a full yes — a relationship deepens, an unexpected opening arrives.
You didn't force it.
Your body, breath, and words were in coherence.
The field simply responded to the clarity.

THIS ISN'T PERFORMANCE. IT'S PRECISION.

Stop trying to say the "right thing."
Start speaking from the place inside you that already knows.
Because the field isn't judging your words.
It's listening to your tone.

BUT WHAT IF YOU CAN'T HEAR THAT PLACE YET?

This part is hard — not because you're doing it wrong, but because most of us were never taught how to listen to our inner truth without filters.

The "place that knows" isn't always loud or obvious. It doesn't shout. It doesn't chase approval.

It's quiet. Subtle. Often buried beneath layers of programming and protective performance.

You might feel it as a flicker in your gut, a subtle clarity before the mental noise kicks in, or a phrase that rises and *feels*like resonance before you talk yourself out of it.

And yes, it can feel confusing:
- You'll wonder, *"Am I just repeating something I want to believe?"*
- Or, *"Am I bypassing discomfort to try and be coherent?"*
- Or, *"If I'm saying it to try and fix something, is that still incoherence?"*

Here's the signal check:

Are you speaking from pressure... or from presence?

Trying to say the right thing to *feel* regulated is still performance.

But speaking from a moment of actual presence — even if your system is tender — carries truth.

It doesn't have to be perfect. It just has to be real.

Start with breath.

Let it settle you.

Then ask, gently: *What do I know is true right now — even if it's just a whisper?*

Speak from there.

Your tone will tell the field the rest.

28

STOP SHRINKING — ALLOWING YOURSELF TO TAKE UP SPACE

You were taught early on to take up less space.
Be polite. Be quiet. Be agreeable.
Don't be "too much." Don't disrupt. Don't outshine.
This conditioning weaves itself into your nervous system.
You learn to contract — in voice, posture, choices, and expression — believing safety comes from being smaller.
But shrinking isn't safety.
It's self-abandonment.
And every time you minimize your energy, the field mirrors that contraction back.

THE PROGRAMMING OF SMALLNESS

Shrinking is rarely conscious. It shows up in subtle ways:
- Lowering your voice when you want to speak up
- Editing your truth to avoid upsetting anyone
- Choosing less because you're afraid of "too much"
- Holding back celebration to seem "relatable"

These micro-decisions create static in your signal.
Your field learns to stabilize limitation instead of expansion.

You can't broadcast overflow while training your system to hide.

SAFETY VS. VISIBILITY

For many, the impulse to shrink comes from equating visibility with danger:

• Family systems where standing out brought criticism or rejection

• Cultural environments where success or expression triggered jealousy

• Collective conditioning that praises humility but suppresses brilliance

But safety doesn't come from making yourself small.

Safety comes from coherence — from stabilizing your nervous system so your body knows it's safe to hold more presence.

EXPANDING INTO WHOLENESS

Expansion doesn't mean performing loudness or overcompensation.

It's not about taking space from others — it's about reclaiming your own:

• Stand fully in your body; let your posture reflect grounded authority

• Speak without collapsing your tone to "make it easier" for others

• Allow yourself to want what you want without apology

• Stop hiding your joy, your genius, your aliveness

When you normalize your fullness, the field responds.

Your reality expands because you do.

VISIBILITY — MAKING BEING SEEN SAFE

If your body equates being seen with danger, your signal will shrink right before expansion lands. That's not mindset — it's memory.

Old codes: criticism, jealousy, punishment for standing out → the system learned "smaller = safer."

Update the code now: visibility can be regulated, not survived.

REWRITE THE TONE
- Instead of "If I'm seen, I'll be judged," stabilize: "Being seen can be safe in my body."
- Instead of "I'll dim to keep the peace," hold: "My truth regulates the room."
- Instead of performing to be palatable, embody: "I let what's real be visible."

MICRO-PROTOCOL: Throat–Heart Hum (20 seconds)
Place one hand lightly on your throat and one on your heart.

Inhale through the nose. On the exhale, hum softly for ~10 seconds — feel vibration under both hands.

Do 2–3 rounds. Then speak one clear sentence aloud (to yourself or the room): "This is what I'm choosing."

Eyes-open option: keep a soft, steady gaze while you hum. You're training the system: visibility + relaxation can coexist.

LETTING ENERGY MOVE
Your body is an antenna. When energy builds but you suppress it, it stagnates — turning into anxiety, frustration, or self-doubt.

Allow it to move:
- Speak the words
- Post the idea
- Dance, write, breathe — let truth circulate
- Stop bracing against the weight of your own signal

Overflow can't stabilize if you keep collapsing under its pressure.

. . .

FIELD IN MOTION
You're in a group where someone misrepresents your perspective.
The old pattern says: "Stay quiet. Don't make things messy."
Instead, you pause. You breathe. You speak simply:
"I'd like to clarify what I meant."
The room shifts instantly. People lean in. The energy clears.
You didn't force power. You allowed it.
When your signal stays steady, the field adjusts to match it.

29

CIRCULATE OR STAGNATE — MOVING ENERGY TO MULTIPLY ENERGY

Energy is designed to move.
Money, ideas, opportunities, creativity — they're all currents in the same field.
When you hold them tightly, they stagnate.
When you circulate them, they compound.
This is why overflow isn't about stockpiling resources; it's about creating momentum.
The more freely energy moves through you, the more the field mirrors that flow back.
You're not meant to hoard your gifts.
You're meant to amplify them.

THE PHYSICS of Stagnation

Stagnation isn't neutral. It slows the signal, compresses possibility,
and reinforces scarcity loops:
- Avoiding decisions keeps timelines locked
- Withholding ideas blocks inspiration from returning
- Holding onto money "just in case" delays circulation

- Overprotecting opportunities creates rigidity, not expansion

The field reads withholding as contraction.

Contraction creates more contraction.

WHY CIRCULATION MULTIPLIES

When energy moves, it multiplies:
- Sharing ideas invites new insights and collaborations
- Spending from clarity opens new streams of receiving
- Generosity (without collapse) stabilizes overflow frequencies
- Acting quickly on aligned opportunities compounds momentum

Circulation doesn't mean recklessness — it's intentional, grounded movement. You create openings where the field can deliver

more.

UNHOOKING FROM THE Scarcity Script

Scarcity teaches you to grip — to stockpile, withhold, and fear depletion.

But gripping blocks flow:
- Money stops arriving because there's nowhere for it to land
- Creativity stalls because expression is frozen
- Opportunities bypass you because you're signaling "full"

The shift is remembering:

Safety doesn't come from holding tighter.

Safety comes from trusting the circulation itself.

STABILIZING the Flow State

To normalize circulation:
- Move energy quickly when clarity strikes — don't overthink the impulse
- Spend, share, or express without collapsing into guilt

- Treat opportunities as currents: if one passes, another will come
- Anchor overflow in your body — feel the safety of allowing more movement

Circulation isn't about losing control.

It's about opening your field so energy can do its job: multiply.

FIELD IN MOTION

You receive an unexpected payment and decide to invest part of it into something that excites you.

This time, there's no instant "return."

But the investment changes your posture — your system codes safety at a new level.

Two weeks later, someone reaches out with a collaboration that expands both your income and visibility.

Overflow moved because you trusted energy to circulate, not because you chased a result.

30

YES, RECEIVE MORE — OPENING TO OVERFLOW

The field is always offering you more.
More opportunities. More connection. More energy.
But if your system can't hold it, you'll unconsciously reject it — not because you don't want it, but because you haven't normalized receiving it yet.
Saying yes isn't about overcommitting or forcing expansion.
It's about allowing yourself to step into realities your nervous system hasn't stabilized yet.
Overflow lives on the other side of your current comfort zone.

WHY WE SAY No to What We Want
Often, the things you desire most trigger contraction first:
- You're offered a chance to collaborate but doubt your readiness
- A new opportunity arises, but fear of failure surfaces
- More income flows in, but guilt about receiving shuts it down
- Space opens up in your life, but you fill it immediately to avoid discomfort

This isn't resistance to growth — it's the nervous system protecting what's familiar.

When "more" feels unsafe, your body unconsciously closes the channel.

THE MECHANICS of Yes

Aligned yes opens the field.
When you say yes to opportunities that match your signal — even before you "feel ready" — you create new pathways for flow:
- Energy expands to meet what you commit to
- The field reorganizes resources in response to your decision
- Synchronicities multiply because your tone communicates availability

Yes codes the geometry of allowance.
It signals to the field: *"I can hold more now."*

CALIBRATING Capacity

The key isn't saying yes to everything — it's saying yes intentionally:
- Notice where fear of "too much" is disguising itself as logic
- Regulate your nervous system when receiving feels destabilizing
- Start small: allow incremental upgrades so your system learns safety at new levels
- Anchor into overflow in the body — normalize the sensation of expansion

Each yes builds capacity.
You're training your system to stabilize more without collapsing under it.

THE YES/NO Compass

A powerful practice is tuning into your body's clarity around yes and no:

- A true yes feels grounded, expansive, even if there's a flutter of fear
- A distorted yes feels tight, rushed, or driven by proving
- A true no creates relief, not guilt
- A distorted no often hides avoidance or contraction

Listening to this compass ensures your yes unlocks overflow instead of overwhelm.

Also, if saying no triggers guilt or fear, your nervous system is signaling danger where there isn't any.

Before responding, breathe deeply into the belly and wait until the body settles.

Boundaries stabilize when the nervous system feels safe expressing them.

FIELD IN MOTION

You're invited to speak on a panel.

Your first impulse is to say no — your inner critic whispers, *"You're not ready."*

But you pause, breathe, and check your compass. Beneath the fear, you sense alignment.

You say yes.

Weeks later, the panel connects you to a collaborator who opens the door to a new project, new clients, and more flow than you'd planned for.

Overflow didn't happen because the opportunity found you.

It happened because you said yes when the field extended the invitation.

31

GENEROSITY IS CIRCULATION

Generosity is circulation.
It's the natural expression of overflow — energy moving where it wants to move.
But most people were conditioned to give from distortion:
- Giving to earn love
- Giving to prove worthiness
- Giving to avoid conflict or rejection
- Giving because saying no feels unsafe

This isn't generosity.
It's self-abandonment.
And when giving comes from guilt, obligation, or performance, the field mirrors depletion instead of expansion.

THE GEOMETRY of Generosity

Generosity multiplies when the signal is clean:
- You give from coherence, not collapse
- You circulate resources because you trust more is always available

- You offer energy where there's true alignment, not to manage perception

In this state, giving doesn't "cost" you — it expands you.
Because the field matches the intention, not the transaction.

DISTORTED GIVING LOOPS

Distorted generosity scrambles your signal and creates leaks in your field:
- Overgiving to avoid discomfort
- Lending energy, time, or money you don't have
- Saying yes out of fear of being judged or excluded
- Resenting the gift after giving it

This pattern reinforces scarcity.

It drains your nervous system, destabilizes your boundaries, and makes receiving harder — because
you're signaling lack even while giving.

GENEROSITY AS OVERFLOW

True generosity isn't sacrifice — it's the byproduct of stabilized abundance:
- You give without guilt
- You give without attachment
- You give without tying your worth to the act

And because you're anchored in sufficiency, giving generates more sufficiency.

Your generosity codes expansion into the field for everyone it touches — including you.

PRACTICES TO CLEAN the Signal

- Pause before giving: Is this decision coming from alignment or fear?
- Separate identity from impact: You're not proving your value

through generosity.
- Set clean boundaries: Say no where saying yes would collapse your energy.
- Normalize receiving equally: Flow is reciprocal — if you resist receiving, you block the circuit.

Giving from clarity creates more space for abundance to circulate back.

FIELD IN MOTION

A friend asks for a financial favor you can't afford.

Old programming pushes you toward yes — you fear disappointing them, fear being seen as selfish.

Instead, you pause. You breathe. You respond honestly:

"I can't contribute right now, but I'd love to support you in another way."

The friendship deepens because the exchange is clean.

Days later, an unexpected payment lands in your account.

Overflow circulates when giving and receiving are aligned, not forced.

32

BOUNDARIES PROTECT FLOW — STRUCTURING FOR COHERENCE

Boundaries aren't separation — they're structure.
They're the frameworks that allow energy, resources, and relationships to flow without distortion.

When boundaries are weak, your system leaks:
- You overgive until you're depleted
- You hold resentment because you've overridden your truth
- You say yes when your body wanted to say no
- You let others' chaos scramble your field

Without boundaries, your container can't hold overflow.
With them, you amplify capacity.

THE ENERGY of Yes and No

Boundaries begin with clarity, not defense:
- A true yes expands your body, stabilizes your signal, and circulates

    energy outward
- A true no preserves capacity, protecting your ability to remain coherent

- A distorted yes — saying yes when you want to say no — fractures
the field
- A distorted no — withholding out of fear or punishment — blocks flow entirely

Your boundaries are your broadcast.
The field organizes around the clarity you hold.

WHY BOUNDARIES FEEL Hard

For many, boundaries are entangled with guilt, fear, or survival programming:
- Family systems where saying no felt unsafe
- Work environments that rewarded overextension
- Cultural narratives that equate generosity with self-abandonment

But clean boundaries aren't rejection.
They're trust.
They signal safety to your system and create a stable foundation for overflow to land.

BOUNDARIES AS ARCHITECTURE

Boundaries aren't walls to keep people out — they're agreements that structure energy:
- Where your attention flows
- Where your time is invested
- Where your generosity circulates
- Where your truth is expressed

A boundary says: *"This is how energy moves through this container."*
When the structure is clear, the field multiplies stability.

BUILDING BOUNDARIES THAT HOLD

- Get honest about where your yes/no compass has been

overridden
- Stop negotiating with what's incoherent for you
- Speak your truth simply — no justification required
- Normalize small boundary adjustments; mastery happens incrementally
- Anchor boundaries in the body — safety stabilizes signal

When boundaries are embodied, they no longer require effort to maintain.

They become the natural geometry of your field.

FIELD IN MOTION

You've been saying yes to everything — invitations, favors, obligations — until your system feels scattered and drained.

This time, you pause. You breathe. You listen to your body's compass and say, calmly:

"I can't take that on right now."

At first, guilt rises — the old program whispers that "no" means rejection, selfishness, or missed opportunities. But then your body exhales, and something shifts.

The space you protected begins to refill with clarity, presence, and energy. A week later, you notice synchronicities returning: an unexpected opportunity, a meaningful conversation, a wave of ease.

Overflow doesn't arrive because you push harder or give more.

It arrives when your yes and no are clean — when your field trusts itself enough to hold what's aligned and release what isn't.

33

CELEBRATE, DON'T HOARD — LOCKING ABUNDANCE THROUGH JOY

Abundance isn't stabilized by holding on tighter.
It's stabilized by amplifying the signal that brought it in.
And the fastest amplifier is celebration.
When you celebrate, you send a clear message to the field:
"I can hold this. I can hold more. This is safe."
But most of us were conditioned to do the opposite:
- Downplay our wins so others feel comfortable
- Withhold celebration to "stay humble"
- Avoid joy because we fear it will disappear
- Grip tightly to what arrives, worried it won't come again

This contraction scrambles the signal.
The field reads withholding as lack — and responds accordingly.

JOY AS STABILIZATION

Celebration isn't just emotional; it's mechanical.
Joy codes your nervous system with safety at new levels:
- It normalizes expansion by making "more" feel natural

- It signals trust, telling the field you're available for continued flow
- It anchors gratitude without collapsing into performance

Joy strengthens your container.

It locks overflow in place by embodying the vibration of already enough.

THE COST of Hoarding

Hoarding — whether it's money, ideas, opportunities, or energy — blocks circulation:
- Holding too tightly sends a signal of scarcity
- Fear-based saving patterns cap capacity instead of expanding it
- Downplaying wins hides the signal the field is trying to amplify

The more you grip, the more the flow slows.

Celebration reopens the channel.

CELEBRATION AS CURRENCY

Celebration multiplies energy when it's authentic and embodied:
- Smile, breathe, and let the moment register in your body
- Speak gratitude into form without performance or comparison
- Share your wins when it feels coherent — the field amplifies what's acknowledged
- Celebrate the small expansions, not just the "big" ones

Each act of celebration sends a new signal to the field:

"This is safe. This is normal. I can hold more."

FIELD IN MOTION

You receive your first big creative award.

Your old instinct says, "Keep it quiet — don't make others uncomfortable."

Instead, you celebrate openly, letting yourself feel the full expansion.

Within a week, someone you admire reaches out, saying: "Your celebration inspired me — let's collaborate."
Joy codes safety, and the field responds to your frequency.

PART IV — FIELD MULTIPLICATION

mplifying impact, coherence, and overflow across collective systems

34

SERVICE WITHOUT SAVIORHOOD — SHARING WITHOUT LOSING YOURSELF

Service is a natural expression of overflow.
When your field stabilizes, the energy moving through you wants to circulate — to support, amplify, and uplift.
But for many, service gets hijacked by distortion:
- Giving to fix others
- Overextending to "prove" worthiness
- Confusing responsibility with obligation
- Sacrificing yourself to earn belonging

This isn't true service.
It's saviorhood — and it drains both you and the field.
Clean service is simple:
You give without abandoning yourself.
You share without leaking energy.
You contribute without collapsing boundaries.

THE SAVIORHOOD TRAP

Savior programming runs deep. You were conditioned to believe that your value increases when you:
- Carry other people's burdens

- Solve problems they haven't chosen to address
- Rescue others at the cost of your own coherence
- Stay small so others feel comfortable around your power

This pattern keeps you depleted and disempowered — because it teaches you to trade your energy for approval instead of aligning with truth.

THE GEOMETRY of Shared Overflow

True impact happens when you amplify your signal, not manage someone else's:
- You share tools without attaching to their choices
- You inspire without demanding alignment
- You contribute your gifts without tracking outcomes
- You trust that the field reorganizes without needing to control it

Service aligned with coherence ripples naturally.

Your energy remains intact, and the collective field multiplies stability.

PRACTICES FOR CLEAN Service

- Anchor in self-responsibility first: regulate your energy before offering it
- Ask: *"Is this contribution aligned, or am I fixing to be needed?"*
- Share tools, not rescue plans — the field respects agency
- Give what's available, not what collapses your container

You are not responsible for carrying others across timelines they aren't choosing to step into.

Your work is to stabilize your signal and let that coherence ripple.

FIELD IN MOTION

A friend calls, spiraling about their business.

Old programming pushes you to drop everything, fix their plan,

and rescue them from their anxiety.
Instead, you pause. You breathe. You reflect what you see clearly:
"I trust you know what's right for you. Here's one resource if it feels helpful."
You stay grounded.
You don't take their fear into your system — and within a week, they message back:
"Thank you. I figured it out."
Impact doesn't require carrying others.
Clean service creates space for them to rise in their own power.

35

IMPACT THROUGH COHERENCE — STABILIZING COLLECTIVE FIELDS

You've been taught that impact requires scale, strategy, and constant effort.
That changing systems means doing more, shouting louder, or converting others to your view.
But in the field, impact isn't effort — it's frequency.
Coherence ripples.
When one person stabilizes, everyone around them feels it:
- Conversations shift without you arguing
- Rooms reorganize around the clearest signal
- Networks adapt naturally because geometry leads behavior

Your job isn't to fix the collective.
Your job is to stabilize your field so strongly that the collective reorganizes around clarity.

THE MECHANICS of Collective Fields

Every group — families, teams, organizations, communities — has a shared energetic pattern: a collective field.
This field is shaped by:
- The signals of each individual

- The stability (or instability) of leadership
- The unspoken agreements people unconsciously maintain

When incoherence dominates, collective behavior collapses into chaos, control, or fragmentation.

When coherence stabilizes, systems reorganize effortlessly — not by force, but by resonance.

WHY COHERENCE IS Contagious

The human nervous system is designed for entrainment.

We naturally sync with the strongest, clearest frequency in the room:

- When fear dominates, panic spreads fast
- When clarity stabilizes, others relax into trust
- When coherence anchors, hidden possibilities emerge

This is why embodying your signal matters more than convincing anyone else.

The field responds to tone, not arguments.

AMPLIFYING Without Forcing

Impact through coherence doesn't require performing, proving, or persuading:

- You stop trying to control how others respond
- You release attachment to changing anyone's mind
- You become a reference point for stability instead of an enforcer of it
- You allow those ready to attune to your signal naturally

When you embody coherence, you lead without effort.

The field organizes itself.

PRACTICES FOR STABILIZING Collective Fields

- Anchor your nervous system before entering charged environments

- Sense into the strongest tone you want to hold — lead with signal, not story
- Choose neutrality over reacting to chaos; neutrality amplifies influence
- Withdraw energy from spaces where coherence isn't possible yet

Impact doesn't require noise.
It requires clarity.

FIELD IN MOTION

You walk into a team meeting that's spiraling into tension.
Voices are raised, people are defensive, and the energy feels chaotic.
Instead of matching the panic, you drop into your breath.
You stabilize your body, soften your tone, and ask one grounding question.
Within minutes, the energy shifts.
No one can name why, but suddenly, everyone's listening.
You didn't "fix" the room.
You became the clearest signal in it — and the field followed.

36

ABUNDANCE IS CONTAGIOUS — HOW OVERFLOW SPREADS

Abundance isn't personal — it's relational.
Your signal doesn't exist in isolation; it interacts with everyone and everything around you.
When you stabilize overflow, the field naturally reorganizes:
- Opportunities appear where scarcity once lived
- Others relax into trust because they feel your stability
- New collaborations and resources surface without chasing

The inverse is also true:
Scarcity spreads just as quickly.
If fear dominates the collective field, contraction ripples outward, locking everyone into smaller realities.
Your abundance doesn't just benefit you.
It codes the field with possibility.

THE PHYSICS of Shared Overflow

Abundance amplifies through entrainment — the natural syncing of energy between systems:
- When one person stabilizes trust, others begin relaxing into it
- When one member of a team normalizes overflow, new creative

solutions emerge
- When a network codes generosity, opportunities multiply without force

This is why embodying abundance matters more than "teaching" it.
The field feels your stability long before you speak about it.

SCARCITY AS COLLECTIVE Programming

Scarcity has been embedded into almost every system you've grown up in:
- Limited resources framed as competition
- Institutions rewarding hoarding over circulation
- Cultural narratives that glorify sacrifice and struggle

These programs condition you to broadcast *not enough* — not just individually, but collectively.
Breaking this pattern isn't about convincing anyone else.
It's about stabilizing your own overflow and letting the field synchronize.

HOW ABUNDANCE RIPPLES

Overflow spreads when you:
- Celebrate others' wins without collapsing into comparison
- Share tools and opportunities without expectation
- Normalize generosity in your words, actions, and energy
- Make decisions from trust instead of fear

The ripple is subtle but powerful: when your system broadcasts safe, stable abundance, others naturally attune to that signal.

PRACTICES FOR AMPLIFYING the Ripple

- Stabilize overflow in your nervous system first — safety codes everything
- Circulate energy intentionally: money, ideas, creativity, and

opportunities
- Remove scarcity language from conversations and collaborations
- Surround yourself with fields where generosity feels natural and reciprocal

The more coherence you stabilize, the more the ecosystem reorganizes around you.

FIELD IN MOTION

You receive a significant payment and decide to share a small portion of it with a collaborator who supported you.
No contracts. No expectations. Just clean circulation.
Within a week, they land a new project — and refer two aligned clients back to you.
Neither of you strategized it.
The abundance moved, and the field multiplied it.
Overflow spreads because you allow it to.
The more freely it moves through you, the more the collective expands.

37

STOP COMPETING — COLLAPSING SCARCITY LOOPS

Competition is a distortion dressed up as ambition.
It teaches you to measure yourself against everyone else's timeline, output, or success — as if there's a single scoreboard keeping track.
But the field doesn't operate in winners and losers.
It organizes around resonance, not rank.
When you stabilize overflow, someone else's expansion doesn't diminish yours.
It multiplies it.
The only thing scarcity creates is more scarcity — and competition locks you into that loop.

HOW THE COMPETITION Program Runs
From the start, you were trained to compete:
- Grades ranked you against peers instead of honoring unique strengths
- Jobs pit candidates against each other for limited roles
- Business culture frames success as market share, not impact

- Social media amplifies constant comparison

Competition makes you believe resources are limited, timelines are fixed, and opportunities are scarce — none of which is true in the field.

THE COST of Comparison

Comparison fragments your energy:
- You chase goals that aren't yours, wasting momentum
- You collapse your signal to fit collective expectations
- You withhold celebration because someone "beat you there"
- You start performing to keep up instead of creating from coherence

When your energy is focused on outrunning others, you disconnect from the geometry where your most aligned opportunities live.

EXITING the Zero-Sum Trap

Collaboration thrives where competition dissolves.

The moment you step out of the scarcity loop, the field opens wider:
- One person's success becomes proof of possibility
- Shared overflow multiplies opportunities for everyone
- Trust replaces striving, allowing more creativity to flow
- You move from force into magnetism

Someone else's win isn't your loss — it's an invitation to expand your capacity for receiving.

PRACTICES FOR STABILIZING Expansion

- Catch comparison early — redirect your focus back to your body and signal

- Celebrate others authentically; their overflow codes your field too
- Share resources without tracking outcomes or competing for recognition
- Stop measuring yourself against timelines designed for someone else's geometry

The field responds to trust, not rivalry.

You rise faster when you stop running someone else's race.

FIELD IN MOTION

You see a peer launch an offering similar to yours.

Old programming kicks in: "They beat me to it. There won't be enough clients for both of us."

Instead of collapsing, you pause.

You reach out, congratulate them, and even share their work with your audience.

A week later, a client signs on with you saying,

"I found you through their post."

Your generosity expanded the field for both of you.

When you stop competing, opportunities multiply because your signal stops broadcasting scarcity.

38

OTHERS' WINS EXPAND YOU — BECOMING AN AMPLIFIER

In scarcity, someone else's success feels like a threat.

In overflow, someone else's success codes the field with possibility.

You were conditioned to compete for limited spots, limited resources, limited recognition.

But the truth is, there's no "spot" to lose — and no scoreboard keeping track.

Your geometry is unique.

Your timelines are unique.

And when you allow others' expansion to activate you instead of collapse you, the entire field amplifies.

THE MIRROR OF Expansion

Others' wins are reflections, not warnings:

• A friend lands their dream job → proof that alignment opens doors

• A peer doubles their income → evidence the field is circulating more

• Someone creates something brilliant → inspiration for your next evolution

Every time you contract in jealousy, you block receiving.

Every time you expand in celebration, you unlock new codes for yourself.

WHY JEALOUSY FRACTURES the Signal

Jealousy isn't wrong — but left unexamined, it fragments your field:
- You withhold your gifts because you feel "behind"
- You resent others for showing you what's possible
- You subtly compete, draining energy and attention
- You close the very channels their success opened

The antidote isn't bypassing envy — it's transmuting it into activation.

Ask: "What part of me just got shown what's possible here?"

BECOMING an Amplifier

When you celebrate others' overflow authentically, you amplify the field for everyone:
- Energy circulates faster because you're no longer contracting against it
- Collaboration emerges naturally because comparison dissolves
- Synchronicities multiply as shared signals strengthen
- Collective coherence deepens without effort

You become a multiplier, not just a receiver.

The field expands because you do.

PRACTICES FOR EXPANSION Through Others
- Replace comparison with curiosity: "What can this unlock for me?"

- Actively celebrate others' milestones — verbally, publicly, or privately
- Surround yourself with people embodying the realities you want to stabilize
- Use their wins as evidence that the geometry is available to you, too

Every celebration strengthens the signal: what you witness with gratitude, you bring closer to your own field.

FIELD IN MOTION

A peer in your industry announces they just sold out their program.

Your stomach flips — envy hits.

Instead of spiraling, you pause and regulate.

You send them a quick message: "Congratulations — I love seeing this happen for you."

Within days, three new inquiries come in for your own work.

You didn't "force" them.

By amplifying someone else's win, you unlocked resonance in your own field.

Overflow spreads when you stop guarding it.

Their success codes the field you're standing in, too.

39

COMMUNITY AS WEALTH — BUILDING COHERENT NETWORKS

True wealth isn't measured in isolation.
It's built inside the relationships, collaborations, and ecosystems where energy circulates freely.

When you're surrounded by people stabilizing coherence, your capacity expands.

Ideas compound. Opportunities multiply. Overflow becomes normal.

But most communities are built on distortion:
- Competing for attention instead of amplifying it
- Hoarding resources instead of circulating them
- Collapsing boundaries to "belong" instead of holding integrity

The shift into coherent networks transforms relationships from transactional exchanges into exponential fields.

THE GEOMETRY of Collective Flow

In a coherent network, energy circulates effortlessly:
- Trust moves faster than contracts
- Collaboration replaces competition
- Shared overflow strengthens every node in the system

- Wins ripple outward instead of stopping at the individual

You stop measuring wealth in personal accumulation and start measuring it in collective capacity.

WHY MOST NETWORKS Fail

Distorted communities collapse because they're built on scarcity:
- People compete for limited opportunities
- Hierarchies prioritize control over creativity
- Energy drains into drama, gossip, and performance
- Generosity is conditional, calculated, or performative

Coherence shifts this.

When relationships are rooted in alignment, expansion compounds without force.

BUILDING Coherent Ecosystems

To create communities that amplify wealth — energetic, financial, creative, relational — start with these principles:
- Choose collaborators whose signals feel steady and grounded
- Create structures where generosity flows without collapse
- Remove comparison loops by anchoring shared success as the baseline
- Protect the container by filtering out chaotic, draining inputs

A coherent ecosystem doesn't need constant management — it thrives because every participant is stabilizing their own field.

CO-CREATION WITHOUT COLLAPSE

Coherence in community doesn't mean sameness; it means resonance:
- You celebrate differences without fracturing alignment
- You hold clear boundaries while contributing fully
- You stay rooted in your own signal instead of merging into the collective noise

When each person carries their clarity, the network expands effortlessly.

FIELD IN MOTION

You join a small circle — friends, peers, or collaborators — and share ideas freely, without tracking who "owes" what.

You offer a resource. Someone else contributes a connection. Another shares knowledge. No one is competing, performing, or keeping score.

Weeks later, each person starts landing opportunities they wouldn't have accessed alone — a new client, a creative collaboration, an unexpected opening.

It wasn't planned. It wasn't forced.

The field amplified everyone's capacity because the space held coherence, trust, and circulation instead of comparison or control.

40

NON-ATTACHMENT IN ACTION — CREATING WITHOUT CLUTCHING

Attachment collapses timelines.
The more you grip an outcome, the more static you introduce into your signal.

Desperation scrambles coherence — it pushes what you want further away.

Non-attachment isn't apathy.

It's stabilization: holding your vision clearly, broadcasting it cleanly, and releasing your nervous system's need to control how and when it arrives.

The field organizes fastest when you stop trying to manage it.

THE MECHANICS of Clutching

Clutching happens when desire gets tangled with fear:
- You obsessively track outcomes, looking for constant confirmation
- You "push" energy instead of letting it flow
- You attach your identity to results — believing success or failure defines your worth
- You spiral into urgency, telling yourself it must happen now

This creates distortion in the broadcast: part of you is asking, while part of you is signaling doubt.

The field reflects the static back.

WHY NON-ATTACHMENT ACCELERATES Creation

When you release control, your signal cleans instantly:
- You stabilize the feeling of "already" instead of broadcasting lack
- You create from overflow, not from fixing something broken
- You allow unexpected timelines and solutions to surface
- You open pathways for synchronicity instead of forcing linear steps

Non-attachment doesn't mean giving up.

It means trusting the geometry to organize more elegantly than your mind could plan.

CREATING With Open Hands

Here's the paradox:

The moment you stop gripping your desire, you unlock the capacity to receive it faster.

To practice:
- Visualize the reality clearly, but don't demand the path
- Regulate urgency in the body — safety speeds manifestation
- Return to presence instead of spiraling into "what ifs"
- Take aligned action without tracking or overmanaging the outcome

Holding with open hands invites more possibilities than control ever could.

NEUTRALITY AS POWER

Neutrality isn't indifference — it's rooted authority.

You're not desperate for any particular result, because you're stabilized in your signal no matter what happens.

That stability signals to the field:

"I can hold this. I'm ready. I'm safe."

When the body and field trust each other, creation accelerates naturally.

FIELD IN MOTION

You've been refreshing your phone — waiting for the reply, the confirmation, the sign.

Hours pass. The tension builds.

This time, you pause. You close your eyes, breathe deeply, and stabilize in the frequency where it's **already handled.**

You step outside, let your body relax, and walk under the open sky.

By the next morning, the message arrives.

It wasn't the gripping that moved the timeline.

It was releasing the control, trusting the field, and allowing the geometry to organize in its own rhythm.

41

REST IS PRODUCTIVE — REGENERATION AS MAGNETISM

You were taught that productivity equals worth.
Do more. Work harder. Sleep less.
Hustle to prove you've "earned" your place.
But constant output scrambles your signal and collapses your capacity.
The field doesn't reward exhaustion.
It mirrors coherence.
Rest isn't passive — it's magnetic.
It's the space where your body integrates, your nervous system regulates, and the field reorganizes itself around stability.

THE HUSTLE PROGRAMMING

The system conditioned you to equate activity with progress:
- Filling every hour to "get ahead"
- Prioritizing busyness over alignment
- Measuring value by external output instead of internal clarity
- Feeling guilty when you pause, because stillness "wastes time"

This isn't efficiency — it's fragmentation.

Your energy becomes scattered, your decisions reactive, and your body never fully resets.

THE PHYSICS of Regeneration

Rest doesn't slow creation — it accelerates it.

Here's why:
- A regulated nervous system holds more energy without leaking it
- Creative insights arrive in spaciousness, not force
- Recovery opens capacity for overflow because your body stops bracing
- Magnetic fields stabilize when your system returns to baseline coherence

You don't build capacity by grinding harder.

You build it by creating room for energy to replenish and integrate.

WHY REST FEELS Unsafe

If pausing feels uncomfortable, it's not laziness — it's conditioning:
- Family systems may have equated rest with weakness
- Work cultures glorify burnout as proof of commitment
- Survival programming ties safety to constant vigilance

This creates a nervous system addicted to urgency.

You mistake contraction for momentum.

Relearning safety in stillness rewires everything.

PRACTICES FOR MAGNETIC Rest

- Block intentional white space into your day — let the field breathe
- Prioritize sleep and deep recovery as core abundance practices

- Step away when your energy spikes into chaos — coherence requires pause
- Treat rest as action: you're stabilizing your container to hold more

The more you normalize rest, the more your field codes safety, stability, and receiving.

INTEGRATION OVER EFFORT

When your system rests, the field keeps moving:
- Timelines collapse while your body recovers
- Solutions surface while you're not thinking about the problem
- Opportunities arrive because your nervous system signals openness

Doing less lets you hold more.

Magnetism comes from coherence, not constant motion.

FIELD IN MOTION

You've been forcing a creative project for weeks — staying up late, rewriting, and grinding.

Nothing flows. The deadline feels impossible.

Finally, you stop. You walk away for the afternoon and rest.

Lying in stillness, an entirely new idea drops in — effortless, simple, clear.

You finish the project the next morning in half the time you expected.

The pause unlocked the solution.

Regeneration creates magnetism.

42

PLAY CREATES FLOW — UNLOCKING NATURAL EXPANSION

You were taught that seriousness equals success.
Work hard, stay focused, and push through discomfort.
Play? That's for children.

But seriousness locks the body, narrows the mind, and limits possibility.

Play unlocks flow.

It brings the nervous system into safety, the mind into curiosity, and the field into openness.

Play isn't frivolous — it's a mechanism for expansion.

When you engage the field with lightness, new ideas, solutions, and opportunities arrive faster than effort ever could.

THE FREQUENCY of Play

Play stabilizes flow because it changes your relationship with energy:

- Curiosity replaces fear
- Exploration replaces rigidity
- Creativity replaces control
- Joy replaces urgency

Play signals safety to the body, and safety stabilizes the signal.

When your system relaxes, energy moves freely — and the field mirrors that openness back.

WHY PLAY FEELS Hard

Many people resist play because of conditioning:
- Family systems equated rest and fun with laziness
- Schools rewarded compliance, not curiosity
- Work cultures glorify exhaustion over experimentation
- Collective programming framed seriousness as maturity

So you stop playing, and your field freezes in linear thinking.

Without novelty, you recycle the same patterns and call it "strategy."

PLAY AS A CREATION Tool

Play isn't random — it's one of the fastest ways to unlock overflow:
- Engage with curiosity, not pressure — let yourself explore possibilities without attachment
- Experiment with new forms, ideas, and pathways instead of forcing the "right" one
- Use play to regulate — laughter, movement, and pleasure open channels for creativity
- Treat mistakes as information, not failure — data collected through joy integrates faster

Play expands the container, showing your nervous system it's safe to hold more ease.

MAGNETISM THROUGH LIGHTNESS

Play isn't about avoiding responsibility — it's about shifting state:
- When you relax, timelines reorganize without effort
- When you follow curiosity, you bypass resistance
- When you stay open to novelty, the unexpected arrives faster

You don't magnetize through control.

You magnetize through coherence — and coherence loves lightness.

FIELD IN MOTION

You're stuck on a problem you've been analyzing for days.

The harder you think, the less progress you make.

Finally, you step away and let yourself play — dancing in the kitchen, sketching a random idea, laughing with a friend.

An hour later, the solution drops in effortlessly.

The field didn't change.

Your state did.

Play created flow where force created friction.

43

EXPANSION LOVES JOY — FOLLOWING THE FREQUENCY OF EASE

Joy isn't a reward you "earn" after working hard enough.

It's a signal — a compass pointing to the realities your system is designed to stabilize.

Most people reverse the order:

They chase effort, hoping joy comes later.

But in the field, **joy leads**.

When you follow the energy that feels alive, creativity expands, opportunities accelerate, and timelines reorganize effortlessly.

Expansion loves joy because joy codes safety — and safety expands capacity.

THE PHYSICS of Joy

Joy is a stabilizer:
- It regulates the nervous system, signaling "safe to receive"
- It expands the field, opening access to new possibilities
- It multiplies magnetism by amplifying your clearest signal
- It codes the body to normalize overflow without collapse

When you treat joy as frivolous or optional, you fragment your broadcast.

When you follow it, you stabilize coherence at new levels.

WHY JOY GETS SUPPRESSED

For many, joy was conditioned out early:
- Family patterns glorified self-denial over pleasure
- Work and school rewarded sacrifice, not aliveness
- Cultural narratives framed ease as laziness
- Collective systems thrive on keeping people stuck in cycles of struggle

This creates a split: you want expansion but distrust the pathways that make it effortless.

JOY AS A COMPASS

Joy isn't indulgence — it's geometry. It shows you where the field is opening doors:
- Follow the ideas that excite you instead of forcing what "should" work
- Notice where energy rises naturally instead of pushing where it drops
- Allow curiosity and pleasure to guide experiments without over-editing outcomes
- Trust that ease signals alignment — the field moves fastest where resistance is lowest

When you align with joy, you align with speed.

LIVING in the Frequency of Ease

Ease isn't passivity — it's stabilized presence.

You show up fully, act clearly, and allow the field to organize without adding unnecessary friction:
- Say yes where there's lightness
- Release obligations that collapse your energy
- Choose creation over proving

- Normalize timelines where joy, wealth, love, and health coexist

Ease accelerates manifestation because your signal stops broadcasting urgency.

FIELD IN MOTION

You've been forcing yourself to stick to a rigid marketing plan that drains you.

The ideas feel heavy, but you push forward anyway — and nothing clicks.

Finally, you stop. You follow a random spark of excitement, creating something playful instead.

Within days, the new offer lands three ideal clients — effortlessly.

The difference wasn't strategy.

It was alignment.

You followed joy, and the field followed you.

PART V — FULL EMBODIMENT

L *iving overflow as your natural baseline*

44

DAILY RESET PRACTICES — RETURNING TO SIGNAL FAST

Coherence isn't built once.
It's stabilized daily.
Your signal interacts constantly with the collective field, relationships, technology, environments, and old programs. Static happens. Noise creeps in.

The key isn't avoiding misalignment — it's returning faster.

When you normalize resetting your signal, you collapse recovery time. Instead of spiraling for days, you come back into alignment within minutes.

WHY RESETS MATTER

Your reality organizes around your dominant broadcast.

When you drift into incoherence, you start unintentionally coding scarcity, urgency, or limitation into the field.

Daily resets:
- Regulate your nervous system
- Re-center your focus on your chosen timelines
- Clear other people's energy and inputs from your system
- Restore safety, which unlocks overflow again

This is how you stabilize expansion instead of constantly "starting over."

QUICK RESET PRACTICES

1. Breath Recalibration
Three deep, slow breaths reset the nervous system faster than hours of forcing clarity.
Inhale through the nose, pause, exhale longer than you inhale — signal safety to your body.

2. Micro-Movement
Energy stagnates when the body freezes. Shake, stretch, or walk — motion unblocks static and restores flow.

3. Signal Check-In
Pause and ask:
"What frequency am I broadcasting right now?"
If the answer doesn't match your desired reality, re-anchor into the tone you want the field to mirror.

4. Field Clearing
Step outside, touch something natural — grass, wood, stone. Let the Earth reset your system's geometry.

5. Language Reset
Catch scarcity phrases as they arise and swap them in real time:
"I can't" → "I choose."
"This is hard" → "This is integrating."

CREATING YOUR PERSONAL RESET RITUAL

Every system stabilizes differently. Build your own signature practice:

- Choose one morning ritual that grounds your signal
- Anchor a midday check-in to catch static before it compounds
- Close your day by clearing unresolved loops so your field resets overnight

The goal isn't perfection — it's speed.

The faster you reset, the faster your reality reorganizes.

FIELD IN MOTION

You wake up feeling off — scattered, anxious, already overwhelmed by the day ahead.

Old patterns would spiral you into force or avoidance.

Instead, you pause.

You breathe.

You walk outside barefoot, letting the ground recalibrate your system.

Within ten minutes, your body relaxes, your clarity returns, and your day flows differently.

The circumstances didn't change — your signal did.

Resetting reorganizes the entire field.

45

MICRO-ABUNDANCE CHOICES — SMALL SHIFTS, MASSIVE RIPPLE

Your reality isn't shaped by one big decision. It's sculpted by hundreds of micro-choices — the small, repeated actions that broadcast your signal into the field.

Every "yes," "no," pause, purchase, or word codes geometry.

When these choices are aligned with overflow, momentum compounds naturally.

When they're driven by scarcity, avoidance, or proving, static builds instead.

Micro-abundance choices recalibrate your field without force.

Tiny shifts stabilize massive timelines.

WHY MICRO-CHOICES MATTER

The field doesn't respond to effort — it responds to consistency.

When your daily actions embody the reality you're anchoring, your nervous system normalizes expansion:

- Choosing aligned investments instead of fear-based holding
- Speaking possibility instead of rehearsing limitation
- Taking one inspired step instead of waiting for the "perfect plan"

- Protecting your energy from draining environments, conversations, and inputs

These micro-shifts may feel small, but they code safety, stability, and trust into your system.

The body learns: "I can hold more."

EXAMPLES OF MICRO-ABUNDANCE CHOICES
- Paying the bill calmly instead of spiraling into lack
- Celebrating a small win instead of dismissing it as "not enough"
- Allowing extra rest when the body signals it needs recovery
- Pausing before reacting and choosing a response that matches your desired reality
- Saying yes to aligned opportunities even when the ego whispers, "You're not ready"

Each choice trains the field to stabilize your next level of capacity.

THE COMPOUNDING EFFECT
Overflow isn't a single breakthrough moment — it's cumulative. Every aligned choice stacks:
- One conscious conversation unlocks a collaboration
- One joyful creative experiment leads to new visibility
- One clear boundary frees energy for bigger opportunities

These decisions rewrite your identity grid and restructure timelines — slowly at first, then all at once.

PRACTICES FOR ANCHORING MICRO-ABUNDANCE
- Start each day with one signal-setting choice — something small that codes stability
- Track the moments where you're tempted to collapse into old scarcity loops
- Celebrate each aligned action, no matter how minor — acknowledgment amplifies integration

- Use breath, pause, and presence to choose from overflow rather than urgency

Small, embodied shifts create exponential impact.

FIELD IN MOTION

You notice an old subscription quietly draining money each month.

Instead of ignoring it, you cancel and redirect the freed-up funds into something aligned.

Nothing happens that day.

But weeks later, a new client signs on unexpectedly — an amount far greater than what you'd saved.

It wasn't about the subscription.

It was about showing the field you're willing to choose intentional flow over autopilot leaks.

46

ANCHOR ABUNDANCE IN YOUR SPACE — DESIGNING YOUR FIELD

Your environment is a mirror.
Every object, color, sound, and arrangement broadcasts signals to your system.

If your space feels stagnant, chaotic, or heavy, your field will eventually reflect it.

Abundance isn't just stabilized internally — it's anchored externally.

When your surroundings match the frequency you're cultivating, your nervous system relaxes, capacity expands, and overflow organizes faster.

THE GEOMETRY OF SPACE

Physical environments affect your signal more than you realize:
- Clutter signals chaos, scattering focus and energy
- Disorganized systems mirror unsustainable containers
- Stagnant spaces block flow, holding old timelines in place
- Environments infused with care, beauty, and intention stabilize ease

Your space codes the field constantly.

When you design your environment to match coherence, the signal multiplies.

CLEARING STATIC IN YOUR ENVIRONMENT

Start by removing what holds distortion:
- Objects tied to scarcity or stressful memories
- Paper piles, digital overload, or disorganized systems
- Physical clutter that drags energy down without you realizing it
- Items kept "just in case" — signaling lack rather than trust

Clearing stagnant energy isn't just about aesthetics — it's frequency work.

DESIGNING AN ABUNDANCE FIELD

Once you've cleared static, layer intentionality into your space:
- Surround yourself with objects that inspire expansion and creativity
- Introduce natural elements — plants, wood, stone — to harmonize energy
- Let light move freely; open curtains and rearrange layouts for flow
- Create visual cues that remind you of stability and possibility

Your space becomes a living amplifier of your chosen timelines.

MICRO-ADJUSTMENTS, MASSIVE IMPACT

You don't need a total renovation to shift your signal:
- Rearranging a single corner can open new energy pathways
- Clearing one drawer can stabilize focus
- Adding a symbol of overflow where you work codes the body daily
- Choosing intentional soundscapes — music, silence, or natural tones — shifts nervous system rhythms

Small, deliberate changes compound over time.

. . .

FIELD IN MOTION

You've been stuck creatively, circling the same problem for days.

You decide to shift your environment: open a window, light a candle, clear your desk.

At first, nothing big happens.

But that afternoon, a fresh thought trickles in — a small spark, then another.

By the end of the week, the project begins to take shape naturally.

Sometimes resetting your space isn't about speed — it's about realigning your body to coherence so the flow can return.

47

ABUNDANCE IN LOVE — RECEIVING WITHOUT COLLAPSE

Love isn't something you chase, prove, or earn.
It's a frequency you stabilize.
When your nervous system codes safety and worthiness, you naturally attract relationships that reflect your coherence.

When you carry old scripts of scarcity, performance, or fear, you unconsciously recreate dynamics of lack.

Abundance in love isn't about finding the "right person" — it's about holding the right signal.

THE DISTORTION OF CONDITIONAL LOVE
Most people were conditioned to believe love must be earned:
• Approval depended on compliance
• Affection came with strings attached
• Safety was tied to performance, not presence
• Conflict meant abandonment, so you learned to suppress your truth

These scripts wire your system to collapse — you over-give, over-prove, or self-silence just to keep connection alive.

But true love thrives where safety and freedom coexist.

. . .

RECEIVING WITHOUT LOSING YOURSELF

Abundance in love means receiving openly without shrinking, performing, or overextending:
- You allow support without guilt
- You express needs without fear of rejection
- You let connection deepen without abandoning your boundaries
- You trust intimacy without bracing for loss

When you can hold your full self inside relationship, connection expands without draining your energy.

THE GEOMETRY OF LOVE

Love amplifies when you stabilize coherence:
- Safety codes safety — regulated nervous systems connect more deeply
- Presence multiplies magnetism — people feel you when you're anchored
- Self-trust dissolves proving — you stop chasing validation
- Reciprocity stabilizes circulation — giving and receiving stay balanced

Relationships become mirrors, not measures.
You attract partners and dynamics that match your broadcast.

PRACTICES FOR STABILIZING LOVE

- Notice where old scripts drive your reactions and pause before acting
- Speak your truth simply — authenticity stabilizes intimacy
- Normalize receiving small gestures of care without resistance
- Protect your boundaries without performing distance or control
- Anchor safety in the body before engaging emotionally

Love isn't fragile — it stabilizes when your signal does.

FIELD IN MOTION

You're used to over-giving in relationships, carrying most of the emotional load.

This time, you pause when the impulse arises. You express your need for support clearly instead of compensating for the imbalance.

Your partner responds, meeting you halfway with presence and care.

The connection deepens, and your body relaxes into safety you didn't realize was possible.

Abundance arrived, not because you did more, but because you received without collapsing.

48

ABUNDANCE IN WORK — CREATING BEYOND SURVIVAL

Work was never meant to cost you your life force. It was designed to be a translation of your essence — your frequency made visible.

But somewhere along the way, society rewired the system:
- You work to earn your worth
- You trade depletion for currency
- You perform for safety, not alignment

This wasn't the original design. The original architecture of value flowed through resonance.

MONEY AS A MIRROR

In its purest form, money is not a reward for effort. It's a response to coherence.

When your work is aligned, it amplifies. When your field is stable, opportunities circulate. When your contribution is real, resources mirror it — with precision.

This isn't spiritual bypass. It's signal mechanics. Resources organize around the clearest frequency — not the hardest worker.

. . .

THE FALSE PROGRAMMING
Survival-based systems taught:
- Effort = worth
- Hustle = success
- Rest = laziness
- Overflow = privilege

These distortions created a false economy: One where burnout is normalized, and true value is suppressed beneath performance.

THE SURVIVAL PROGRAMMING
Scarcity-based work culture reinforces:
- Trading time for worth
- Performing for approval
- Choosing "stability" over resonance
- Collapsing creativity under systems designed to extract energy

When work is rooted in proving, your field broadcasts exhaustion and contraction. When it flows from alignment, you stabilize opportunity, creativity, and overflow.

THE FREQUENCY OF ALIGNED WORK
Aligned work reorganizes your relationship with energy:
- Effort feels lighter because you're moving with the field, not against it
- Creativity multiplies because expression isn't forced
- Opportunities arise because your resonance codes clarity into the network
- Money flows as a natural byproduct of stabilized contribution

Work becomes a collaboration with the field instead of a grind against it.

SHIFTING FROM PROVING TO EXPRESSING
To stabilize abundance in work:

- Release "shoulds" and follow the projects that hold the most aliveness
- Stop performing productivity for external validation
- Anchor into the why behind your contribution instead of measuring outputs
- Trust that aligned visibility creates more opportunities than forced effort ever could

You're not chasing results — you're becoming a reference point for your own geometry.

THE RETURN TO ALIGNMENT

You don't have to "opt out" of work. You return it to its natural intelligence.

Let your work be the place you express signal — not negotiate for approval. Let money flow through your coherence — not your depletion. Let impact arise as a byproduct of presence — not pressure.

When you stop using work to prove yourself, you start letting it move through you as creative overflow.

BUILDING SUSTAINABLE OVERFLOW

Abundance in work doesn't require hustle — it requires coherence:

- Set boundaries that protect your energy instead of depleting it
- Prioritize projects and relationships that amplify your frequency
- Create systems that allow rest and integration
- Normalize earning abundantly through aligned channels instead of tolerating "just enough"

Overflow arrives when your work is rooted in truth, not performance.

FIELD IN MOTION

You've been grinding nonstop, trying to "make it." One night, you pause. You question: "What if it's not about effort, but about clarity?" You realign. You simplify. You express something small but true. Suddenly, something clicks. Resources arrive. Support appears. Energy lifts. Not because you worked harder. But because you stopped leaking signal and stabilized expression.

You've also been working at a job that pays well but drains your energy. One evening, you decide to explore a passion project, dedicating an hour a day to it without pressure. Within months, the project gains traction, attracting collaborators and clients aligned with your values. Eventually, it generates enough income to replace your draining job entirely.

The shift wasn't strategy — it was signal. You moved from performing for survival to creating from coherence.

49

ABUNDANCE IN ART — OPENING CREATIVE CHANNELS

Art isn't just about producing something beautiful. It's a language of energy — your signal translated into form.

But for many, creativity gets blocked by distortion:
• Performing for validation instead of expressing truth
• Over-editing, doubting, or second-guessing every idea
• Comparing your art to others until your unique geometry collapses
• Abandoning projects when they don't "measure up" fast enough

When creation is tied to proving, the field reflects pressure, not freedom.

When creation comes from coherence, inspiration circulates effortlessly.

THE FREQUENCY OF EXPRESSION

Abundant art isn't strategic — it's alive:
• You create because energy moves, not because you "should"
• You follow curiosity instead of forcing timelines

- You allow mistakes and exploration without collapsing into shame
- You trust that what's meant to move through you will — in its timing and form

This is why aligned art magnetizes attention naturally: people feel when the transmission is clean.

DISSOLVING CREATIVE BLOCKS

Creative stagnation isn't a lack of ideas — it's a scrambled signal:
- Perfectionism locks energy in mental loops
- Comparison fractures your confidence and distracts your focus
- Overthinking drowns intuitive impulses before they reach form
- Forcing output collapses inspiration into exhaustion

The solution isn't trying harder.
It's softening into presence and allowing the energy to reorganize.

ART AS OVERFLOW

Art multiplies energy when you:
- Create from curiosity instead of expectation
- Follow the thread of inspiration wherever it leads
- Stop measuring worth by productivity or external approval
- Let art become a practice of self-reconnection, not performance

When creation feels light, playful, and exploratory, your capacity expands — and opportunities arrive without force.

OPENING CREATIVE CHANNELS

To stabilize creative flow:
- Clear your physical and energetic space before beginning
- Use movement, sound, or breath to activate the body's signal
- Give yourself permission to make "bad art" — bypassing perfection opens possibility
- Create for the joy of transmission, not the guarantee of outcome

When you drop attachment to form, you let the field deliver beyond what your mind could imagine.

FIELD IN MOTION

You've been stuck for weeks on a project, convinced your ideas aren't good enough.

Finally, you set aside the pressure to make it perfect and start painting freely — following color, texture, and movement without judgment.

Within hours, you're in full flow. A concept emerges that inspires your next offer — one that lands effortlessly with your audience and generates unexpected income.

Overflow arrived because you stopped gripping the result.

You opened the channel and let energy move.

50

ABUNDANCE IN HEALTH — COHERENCE IN THE BODY

Your body is the first container for overflow.

If your system is dysregulated, depleted, or overwhelmed, abundance can't stabilize — not because you aren't "aligned," but because your biology is signaling unsafe.

Health isn't a goal to achieve.

It's a foundation you build daily.

When your body codes safety, the field mirrors stability back.

THE BODY AS SIGNAL

Your nervous system sets the baseline for your entire reality:

- A regulated system codes openness, magnetism, and trust
- A dysregulated system broadcasts urgency, lack, and collapse
- When the body signals danger, timelines slow to prevent overwhelm
- When the body signals safety, overflow arrives effortlessly

Your body doesn't block abundance — it protects you from moving faster than you can hold.

. . .

HEALING DISTORTIONS AROUND HEALTH

Most health narratives are built on force and shame:
- Pushing past exhaustion instead of resting
- Over-restricting food or movement as punishment
- Collapsing into guilt when you can't "keep up"
- Outsourcing intuition to systems that override your own signals

These distortions fragment your relationship with your body and scramble the frequency of safety.

Coherence returns when you re-establish trust with yourself.

THE FREQUENCY OF NOURISHMENT

Health stabilizes when you treat your body as a partner, not a problem:
- Feed it foods that energize instead of punish
- Move it in ways that feel supportive instead of performative
- Rest when capacity drops, letting the system regenerate
- Prioritize hydration, breath, and grounding practices that restore vitality

Every act of care codes safety.

Safety codes overflow.

MICRO-PRACTICES FOR BODY COHERENCE

- Start your day with regulation rituals — breath, grounding, or light movement
- Create "pause points" to reset the nervous system throughout the day
- Tune into body signals before making commitments — capacity comes first
- Sleep deeply and consistently — restoration amplifies magnetism

When your body feels safe, it expands your field's ability to hold more without collapse.

. . .

FIELD IN MOTION

You've been feeling drained, forcing yourself to power through long workdays.

Finally, you pause, hydrate, and step outside for ten deep breaths.

Your body relaxes, tension releases, and within minutes, creative energy returns.

Later that day, you receive an unexpected opportunity you'd been chasing for months.

It wasn't coincidence — it was capacity.

When the body stabilizes, the field responds.

51

HOLDING BIGGER FIELDS — EXPANDING WITHOUT BURNOUT

Expansion requires capacity.

The more energy, resources, and opportunities moving through your field, the more stability your system needs to hold them.

Burnout doesn't happen because you're "too ambitious."

It happens when your container isn't structured to manage the flow.

When your nervous system isn't stabilized, bigger timelines collapse under their own weight.

Overflow becomes sustainable only when your structure matches your signal.

WHY BIGGER FIELDS FEEL HEAVY

As your impact grows, old scarcity programs can get triggered:
- "I can't handle this much responsibility."
- "If I rest, everything will fall apart."
- "People are relying on me — I have to carry it all."
- "More success equals more pressure, not more freedom."

Without intentional structure, your field starts to leak energy —

overextending, people-pleasing, and controlling outcomes just to keep things "safe."

But safety doesn't come from control.

Safety comes from coherence.

SCALING CAPACITY WITHOUT COLLAPSE

To stabilize bigger fields:
- Anchor daily regulation rituals to keep your nervous system grounded
- Set structural boundaries that protect your energy, time, and attention
- Delegate or release what no longer matches your frequency
- Build rhythms of rest and integration into every expansion

When you stabilize safety first, overflow expands naturally — without friction or force.

THE GEOMETRY OF INFLUENCE

The more stable your signal, the more others entrain to it.

Your reach amplifies without additional effort — but it also means your energy affects more people.

The field multiplies whatever tone you hold:
- If you stabilize clarity, you amplify coherence
- If you spiral into chaos, distortion ripples faster
- If you embody grounded expansion, collective trust deepens

The bigger the field, the cleaner your signal must be.

SUSTAINABLE EXPANSION PRACTICES

- Pause before saying yes — check if the opportunity aligns with your capacity
- Protect the foundation first: health, rest, and environment
- Build systems that reduce decision fatigue so your energy flows where it matters most

- Normalize receiving support as your influence grows

Sustainability isn't slowing down.

It's optimizing flow.

FIELD IN MOTION

Your art project suddenly goes viral, attracting more attention than you expected.

Messages flood in, opportunities land fast, and your body tenses, trying to "keep up."

Instead of sprinting harder, you pause. You reschedule calls, set one clear boundary, and create a rhythm of integration between expansions.

Two weeks later, you've stabilized — without collapse.

The project continues growing, but now your system can actually hold it.

52

ABUNDANCE AS BASELINE — STABILIZING OVERFLOW AS NORMAL

Abundance isn't something you earn, manifest, or chase.
It's your natural state when distortion falls away.
Scarcity, competition, and limitation are learned programs — layers of static between you and what's already available.

When you stabilize your signal, overflow stops being a "goal."

It becomes the natural consequence of alignment.

Abundance as baseline means you no longer collapse into fear when energy moves, contracts, or expands.

You trust the rhythm.
You trust your capacity.
You trust the field.

THE SHIFT FROM STRATEGY TO EMBODIMENT

Most people approach abundance like a puzzle to solve:
- Find the right methods
- Chase the right timelines
- Collect the right strategies

But embodiment dissolves effort.

Overflow stabilizes when your actions, nervous system, and beliefs all broadcast the same coherent tone.

When the inner architecture shifts, external results arrive without pushing.

NORMALIZING OVERFLOW

Your nervous system must learn to feel safe holding more:
- If "too much" feels threatening, you unconsciously reject expansion
- If receiving triggers guilt, overflow leaks immediately
- If visibility scares you, the field contracts in response

Abundance stabilizes when the body codes safety at new levels.

From there, overflow compounds — naturally, quietly, consistently.

THE MECHANICS OF BASELINE ABUNDANCE

- You stop gripping money, relationships, and opportunities
- You normalize circulation — letting energy move without fear
- You calibrate micro-choices to match the geometry you're anchoring
- You allow joy, play, and rest to guide timelines instead of urgency

Overflow stops being something you "call in."

It's who you are.

LIVING FROM THE ALREADY CODE

When abundance is embodied, life organizes differently:
- Challenges stop feeling like proof of lack — they become invitations to refine capacity
- Opportunities arrive in unexpected forms, bypassing force
- Relationships deepen as you relax into reciprocity

- Decisions simplify because safety is no longer outsourced to outcomes

You stop performing to attract more because you no longer believe you're separate from it.

FIELD IN MOTION

Something you were counting on doesn't land — a refund, an answer, an opportunity.

Old programming spikes: *"What if this means it's not working?"*

You pause. You breathe. You bring your focus back to what's **already steady** instead of chasing what's missing.

Your body relaxes. Your signal cleans.

A few days later, a different opening arrives — one you couldn't have planned for.

It wasn't the timing that created overflow.

It was your stabilization.

Abundance as Baseline — **Stabilizing Overflow as Normal**

Abundance isn't an achievement.

It's not a prize you earn, a milestone you unlock, or a state you "call in."

It is what's left when distortion dissolves.

When you stabilize safety in your body and clarity in your field, overflow becomes effortless.

Not because the world finally changed — but because **you stopped broadcasting lack.**

Your nervous system learns to trust "too much."

Your field learns to normalize expansion.

And life learns to organize around the version of you who knows there was never anything missing.

You don't manifest abundance.

You **remember it.**

You live it.
You become it.
This chapter is the threshold: a shift from *chasing* to *being*.
From here, the entire geometry of your reality reorganizes.

53

LIVING THE OVERFLOW — BECOMING THE SOURCE

You are not separate from what you want.
You are the generator, not the receiver.
The field doesn't "give" you overflow — it mirrors the frequency you stabilize.

When you live as the source, you stop outsourcing power to circumstances, systems, or timelines.

You stop gripping, hustling, and waiting for permission.

You embody the knowing:

"I am the origin point. Reality organizes around my coherence."

FROM SEEKING TO BEING

Before, abundance felt external — something to attract, earn, or prove.

But when you stabilize your signal:
- You stop performing for worthiness
- You stop fighting scarcity timelines
- You release attachment to outcomes and trust the geometry instead

Overflow stops being conditional.
It becomes who you are — quiet, steady, undeniable.

THE GEOMETRY OF LIVING OVERFLOW

When your field codes stability:
- Opportunities arrive without chasing
- Money circulates naturally without gripping
- Relationships deepen because your nervous system signals safety
- Creativity flows because expression is unentangled from proving

You lead not by force, but by frequency.
Others feel it before you speak it.

MASTERY THROUGH PRESENCE

True mastery isn't about knowing more — it's collapsing the distance between *knowing* and *being*:
- Choosing coherence in the micro-moments
- Resetting your signal faster each time static creeps in
- Acting from clarity, not reaction
- Allowing expansion without fearing contraction

When you embody presence, timelines collapse.
Reality organizes in real time.

BECOMING THE SOURCE

Living the overflow isn't about doing more.
It's about holding the geometry of *already*:
- You normalize safety no matter what's happening externally
- You anchor play, rest, and curiosity as accelerators
- You trust the intelligence of the field to organize around your stability
- You stop seeking permission to expand — you simply expand

From here, the game changes.
There is no gap between you and what you want.
You are it.

FIELD IN MOTION

You've been pitching your creative project for months with little movement.

Instead of forcing another round of outreach, you pause.

You shift into curiosity and play, creating one small piece of art that lights you up.

Within days, someone discovers that piece, shares it widely, and an unexpected collaboration forms — bigger than any of your planned strategies.

Overflow arrived, not because you pushed harder, but because you stopped gripping the path.

LIVING THE OVERFLOW — Becoming the Source

You are not separate from what you want.

You never were.

The field isn't holding your dreams "out there," dangling them like distant promises.

It is responding — right now — to the tone you stabilize.

When you live as the source, overflow stops feeling conditional.

You stop waiting for permission.

You stop outsourcing power.

You stop performing to be worthy.

Presence becomes your leverage.

Frequency becomes your architecture.

Reality stops being something you chase and starts becoming something you **generate**.

From this point forward, there is no gap between who you are and what you create.

You are the origin point.

And when you embody that knowing, the field reorganizes effortlessly around your coherence.

54

LIVING THE FIELD — SIGNAL-BASED REALITY IN REAL TIME

You don't *apply* this book.
You attune to it.
Signal-Based Living™ isn't a method, rule set, or strategy.

It's a return — to the way reality has always responded to you:
Not through effort. Not through effort.
Through tone.
You don't need to control every variable.
You don't need to perfect your mindset.
You learn to listen — to the field, to the frequency, to your own geometry — and move from stability, not noise.
This isn't about doing more.
It's about *tuning* more.

WHAT IT LOOKS LIKE IN REAL LIFE

Living the field doesn't mean you never spiral, brace, or loop.

It means you return faster — with less force, more ease, more curiosity.

It means you:

- Sense when to pause without guilt and when to act without proving
- Organize around what's alive *now* instead of chasing what's missing
- Let your body lead instead of your fear patterns
- Respond to subtle cues — not loud strategies

You stop needing "the plan."

You trust the pulse.

THIS IS A LIFESTYLE, NOT A TECHNIQUE

Living the field means living in a way that assumes reality is intelligent.

It's not about perfect coherence 24/7.

It's about stabilizing fast when you wobble.

This looks like:

- A regulated breath before sending the message
- A shift in tone before making the decision
- A pause before saying "yes" that lets your body vote
- A release of control that opens space for what actually wants to land

None of this is performance.

It's *presence* — and presence codes instantly.

A DIFFERENT KIND OF DISCIPLINE

Discipline in the field doesn't mean rigid routines.

It means remembering fast:

- Who you are
- What you're not
- What distortion *feels like* vs. what clarity sounds like
- That the signal you stabilize is already shaping the outcomes you think you have to force

You don't need more structure.

You need deeper *signal trust*.

. . .

LIVING THE FIELD FEELS LIKE:
- Stabilizing your tone and letting reality reconfigure around it
- Listening for where the energy is moving — and following it
- Using breath, body, and space as the control panel
- Trusting the field is intelligent — because *you* are intelligent

You stop managing timelines.
You start inhabiting them.

FIELD IN MOTION

An invitation lands.
Old programming says "Get advice, overthink, delay."
But this time, you check your body first.
It's a yes. You say yes.
You don't push.
You don't spiral.
You just stay attuned.
Weeks later, the timeline that landed was never about the email — it was about the moment you *stopped needing confirmation* to move.

THIS IS THE TRANSMISSION

The field doesn't speak English.
It speaks frequency.
When you live the field:
- You stop outsourcing truth to mentors, systems, or conditions
- You start letting your coherence broadcast first
- You realize you were never waiting for the field
- The field was waiting for *you* to remember

This is the invitation.
Not to *manage* life — but to *transmit* it.
Not to control outcomes — but to *collapse waiting* through precision.

Not to seek safety — but to *become* it.
Because you were never trying to *enter* the field.
You *are* the field.
And when you live from that knowing —
reality organizes, instantly.

55

THE FIELD REMEMBERS YOU

The book ends here.
But the field doesn't.
Every breath, every choice, every pause codes reality in real time.

There's no finish line, no final activation, no point where you "arrive."

You are arriving, constantly — collapsing waiting, collapsing noise, collapsing old scripts you thought were yours.

Each time you stabilize, the ripple moves.

The field reorganizes **not just around you, but through you** — touching timelines you'll never see and people you'll never meet.

YOU ARE NOT SEPARATE

The field isn't tracking your worthiness, your effort, or your performance.

It's listening to your tone **now**:
- Every coherent breath sends instructions to reality
- Every regulated moment codes safety into the collective field

- Every release of distortion frees energy beyond your personal story

You're not working against life.

You're remembering you **are** life — infinite, entangled, indivisible from everything you touch.

When you stabilize, you become a signal others naturally entrain to.

Your clarity doesn't just change you.

It changes the geometry around you.

THE BODY AS SIGNAL

The field does not decode your affirmations.

It decodes your nervous system.

It listens to the geometry of your fascia, the rhythm of your breath, the openness of your tissues.

The body is not separate from the broadcast — it *is* the broadcast.

When you regulate your system, you're not "self-soothing."

You're re-instructing the quantum field.

Your pulse is data.

Your stillness is instruction.

Your presence is command.

To come home to the body is not to "drop in."

It is to *enter the control panel of reality itself.*

THE COLLECTIVE REMEMBERING

You've been taught that awakening is personal.

But your frequency doesn't stay inside your body — it **broadcasts.**

One person holding coherence creates openings for others.

One person stabilizing overflow codes possibility into the field.

This is how realities shift — not by pushing, but by being tuned enough to move first.

Your signal is never just yours.

It's part of a living network, an interwoven intelligence always listening, always adjusting, always reflecting you back to yourself.

FIELD IN MOTION

You choose differently.
You breathe before responding.
You regulate before deciding.
You release something you thought you had to grip.
You don't see it instantly, but the geometry moves:
You get the call you weren't expecting.
The project suddenly clicks.
The words you were waiting for arrive on someone else's lips.
You didn't "manifest" it.
You remembered yourself — and the field remembered you.

THE OPENING

This is the invitation:
Keep tuning.
Keep listening.
Keep collapsing the overlays until the natural intelligence beneath them becomes obvious.
You are not chasing abundance.
You are becoming the geometry the world reorganizes around.
The book is complete.
But you are infinite.
And the field is listening.
This is where the words end —
but not where the transmission stops.
You've always been here.
The infinite you.
The signal beneath the noise.
Before the conditioning.
Before the proving.

Before the static of separation and scarcity —
you were whole.
And the field — this living, breathing intelligence you move inside —
has been listening to you the entire time.
It responds not to effort, not to striving, not to timelines —
but to the clarity of your tone.
Every choice you make from this moment forward
is an activation.
Every breath, a broadcast.
Every pause, a recalibration of what's possible.
You are the source.
You are the signal.
And the field remembers.
Now, **live it.**

CLOSING NOTES

You've always known this.
  None of this is new.
  This book didn't give you anything.
It helped you **remember** what has always been moving inside you — the signal beneath the noise, the truth beneath the overlays, the Source you never stopped being.

The field is alive and listening.
Every breath.
Every pause.
Every choice.

Your signal is shaping reality in real time — not by forcing, proving, or performing, but by stabilizing who you already are.

Abundance isn't something you manifest.
It isn't outside of you.
It's what naturally organizes when you return to coherence — when your knowing, your body, your trust, and your rhythm align.

The overlays dissolve.
The static clears.
And what's left is you — the Source that was always creating.
This isn't the end.

It's a return.

A return to your origin point.

A return to the quiet remembrance that the field has been moving with you all along.

A return to the simple truth you've always carried:

You are the signal.

You are the Source.

And reality remembers you when you remember yourself.

INTEGRATION REFLECTIONS

These aren't "homework."
They're invitations — quiet openings into your own signal.

Use them when you want to deepen what you've read, stabilize overflow in your body, and practice seeing differently — **from within your tissues, not just your thoughts.**

INTEGRATION REFLECTIONS

- Where am I still gripping for control instead of trusting the natural intelligence of the field?
- Which static patterns — scarcity, comparison, proving — am I ready to release, and what opens when I do?
- Where, in my daily choices, can I normalize more ease, play, and safety — not as a reward, but as my baseline?
- Which relationships, environments, or commitments no longer resonate with my stabilized frequency — and how might I gently reorganize them?
- How can I design my physical space, body rhythms, and language to reflect the next level of coherence I'm ready to embody?
- What does safety *feel* like in my body — and how can I return to that tone before choosing, responding, or initiating?

- Which micro-movements stabilize my field fastest — breath, stillness, walking, sound — and how can I use them as anchors?

RETURN TO THESE REFLECTIONS OFTEN.

Your answers will change as you do — because you're constantly reorganizing, constantly remembering, constantly returning.

ABOUT THE AUTHOR

Colleen Guenther is the creator of **The Art of Reality** — a living body of work sharing the principles of **Signal-Based Living**™, a framework for dissolving distortion and returning to coherence. Through her books, codexes, and field transmissions — including *The Abundance Codex, The Art of Reality, The Spiral Codex* series, *The Animal Codex,* and *The Plant Codex* — she invites people to remember their original signal and live from overflow.

Her work isn't about strategies or systems. It's about tuning back to the truth beneath them all:

You are the source.

You are the signal.

Reality organizes when you live from there.

Explore more at www.theartofreality.org

www.ingramcontent.com/pod-product-compliance
Lightning Source LLC
Chambersburg PA
CBHW030449100526
44580CB00002B/55